HANGED AT YORK

STEPHEN WADE

The
History
Press

First published 2008

The History Press Ltd
The Mill, Brimscombe Port
Stroud, Gloucestershire, GL5 2QG
www.thehistorypress.co.uk

Reprinted 2011

British Library Cataloguing in Publication Data.
A catalogue record for this book is available from the British Library.

ISBN 978 0 7509 5042 8

Typesetting and origination by The History Press Ltd.
Printed in Great Britain by Marston Book Services Limited, Oxford.

CONTENTS

ACKNOWLEDGEMENTS

I would like to thank many people who helped me with the preparation of this book. Thanks are due to Michelle Petyt and Melanie Baldwin at York Castle Museum, who very kindly helped me with the process of unearthing some of these harrowing stories. Also, York Art Galleries & Museums Trust are to be thanked for permission to use the Rowlandson print of 'Mary Evans Hanged at York' on page xv. In terms of secondary sources, books such as this would be much more difficult to produce were it not for the labours of two crime historians in particular who have made it their business to compile reference works and casebooks in this area of research: these are Steve Fielding and David Bentley. The former's work, *The Hangman's Record*, has been invaluable, and the latter's collection, entitled *The Sheffield Hanged 1750–1854*, is a marvellous source. Staff at Whitby Archive Heritage Centre were also very helpful.

INTRODUCTION

York, above all English cities, can claim to be the location of the most gallows. It might be called the 'city of scaffolds', with some justification. Over the centuries, since the first properly recorded hangings in the thirteenth century, there have been several hanging places, both in the city and in its environs. In 1867, William Knipe published *A Criminal Chronology of York Castle*, and he began at 1 March 1379. But the history of York gallows goes back much further, with references to places other than the castle.

Between 1135 and 1140, four charters were given to the Priory of the Holy Trinity by King Stephen, and these included the right to establish gallows. This was known as 'the thieves' gallows' and was most likely sited near the Knavesmire gates. Then, in 1379, there was a meeting of the bailiffs of the city with the Grand Jury members to decide on a place to erect city gallows. There was already a gibbet post on the Knavesmire so that was chosen: gallows were made on the roadside on Hob Moor, put in place on 7 March 1379, and the place became known as the York Tyburn, named after the London Tyburn (near Marble Arch today) which had been in place since 1220.

The ostensible reason for deciding on such an act was an escalation of riotous and violent confrontations between the citizens and the monks of St Mary's. But there was already another gallows on Foss Bridge and another one at the Horsefair – the junction of the Haxby and Wigginton roads. The roots of these gallows, supervised by religious authorities, lie in the old concept of *Infangtheof*, a power to deal with malefactors in their ecclesiastical area. There was also the old idea of Church personnel having a right to 'seek out and determine' breaches of the law.

The later history of hangings in York embraces some of the most turbulent periods in English social and political history. In 1536, for instance, the Pilgrimage of Grace, in which a mass movement of dissatisfaction against Henry VIII's dissolution of the religious houses took place, one of the leaders, Robert Aske, was hanged at York. Again, when the lords of the north revolted against the sovereign in 1569, the suppression and retribution was severe and merciless. When this failed, the Earl of Sussex led the move to retribution, and as T.P. Cooper has written, the rebels were hunted down relentlessly:

> Hundreds are said to have been executed at Durham, and in Richmondshire and other parts of the North Riding . . . On Good Friday, 27 March 1570, Simon Digby of Askew, John Fulthorpe of Iselbeck, Robert Pennyman of Stokesley and Thomas Bishop of Pocklington, gentlemen, all of whom had taken an active part in the rebellion, were conveyed from York Castle to the Knavesmire, and were hanged, beheaded and quartered.

Many unfortunates hanged at York have remained in total obscurity and we will never know their names; many others are recorded but their offences are merely listed, and there is no narrative added to provide a full account of the crime and its trial. Felons were hanged in all areas of the city, and only with the early modern period have we had substantial records, and those from York Castle itself. At the end of the seventeenth century and into the Georgian years, there was a period of building during which the various judicial and penal establishments in the Eye of York around Clifford's Tower were completed. Between 1701 and 1705, the

Foss Bridge, a place of execution in the medieval period. (Author's collection)

new county gaol was built and then, between 1773 and 1777, the great architect John Carr designed the assize courts. By 1780 there was also a new prison for women in the area.

York Castle comes to dominate the criminal justice process of Yorkshire right up to the switch of the Assizes to Leeds in 1864. The new prison was built between 1825 and 1835, with radiating wings and a governor's house. Sent to York for trial, criminals of the Georgian and Victorian period were imprisoned and sometimes executed. The long list of crimes and the social changes related to the crimes cover such massive historical processes as the Luddite unrest of 1812–16; Chartist prisoners from the 1840s; 'domestic' murderers; coiners; sheep stealers; fraudsters; and many others. There were poachers who had killed gamekeepers, sacked labourers who burned their masters' hayricks, insane people who took a knife or axe to a partner or companion, women poisoners, and perhaps most poignant of all, the young women who had committed the crime of 'child-murther' – until 1922 simply a version of murder, rather than the crime of manslaughter it became after that date.

Until 1801, the Tyburn tree, also known as the 'three-legged mare' on the Knavesmire, was the destination of these felons, from the infamous Dick Turpin in 1739 to the obscure drunks and men of violence; but after that date the hanging place became the 'new drop' made at the south-west end of the Assize Courts, facing St George's Field. The crowds that had once gathered on the Knavesmire to watch criminals die now filled St George's Field to see the gruesome spectacle, up until 1868 when public executions were abolished. The new drop was first used on 28 August 1802, after the last man, Edward Hughes, had been hanged on the Knavesmire in 1801. In 1805, a bank of earth was made which would enclose the scaffold in order to keep spectators as a distance and avoid accidents through the crowds becoming unruly.

Other gallows gradually fell into disuse, including the one at the City Gaol on Ouse Bridge, which had existed since 1578 and had been rebuilt in 1724. But in 1801 a new gaol was made which was to deal with capital offences committed within the city itself; some land near the Baile Hill was selected for this. The main outside wall fronted a lane leading from Skeldergate to Bishopshill Senior Church. Cromwell Road today is the site of this. When there was to be a hanging, a scaffold was erected outside the wall by the Baile Hill and an opening was made in the wall for the condemned person to go through.

Right: *Clifford's Tower, where executions took place, also the site of a mass murder of Jews in the thirteenth century.* (Author's collection)

Below: *Plan of the Assize Courts, from an 1822 commission.* (Parliamentary papers)

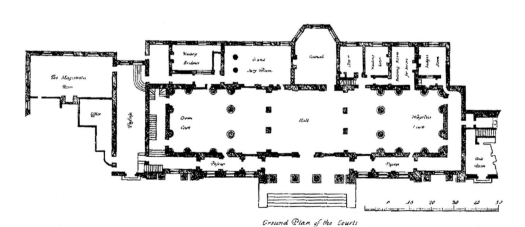

Ground Plan of the Courts

PLAN OF THE ASSIZE COURTS.

The shrine in The Shambles of Margaret Clitherow, a woman pressed to death, an earlier method of execution for some offences. (Author's collection)

The Privy Council made the decision to move the West Riding Assizes from York to Leeds in 1864 and York remained the County Assizes for the East and North Ridings of Yorkshire. The City Gaol in Gaol Lane continued to be in use until 1869.

The backdrop to this long line of executions was the huge body of statutes embodying capital punishments in the criminal law of the land. By the year 1800, there were over 200 such offences. In 1752, there was an act passed which expressed the spirit of sheer inhuman suppression behind these laws; the wording explained what would happen to murderers condemned to the scaffold: '. . . persons convicted of murder should be executed on the next day but one after their sentence of death has been passed, and that their bodies should be given to the surgeons to be anatomised, or hung in chains; and further, that the prisoners should be fed on bread and water only after being sentenced . . .'

The hangings were the focus of much commercial activity as well; street tradesmen would sell chapbooks and ballads, and even copies of supposed 'last dying speeches' on the day of the execution. A chapbook printed in 1820, entitled *Cries of York*, has the refrain:

> Come buy a true calendar
> Of prisoners in the castle drear,
> Come buy a calendar;
> Their crimes and names are set down here
> 'Tis truth I do declare.

The hangmen of York were usually convicts, men who took on that unenviable task in order to save their own lives or to avoid a term of transportation to Van Dieman's Land. Most notorious of these was William Curry, a man whose career included several drunken bunglings on the scaffold; he will figure in many of the following gallow tales. Curry was a mysterious figure; he was also known as William Wilkinson, a labourer from Thirsk, who had crossed to the wrong side of the law and had a death sentence passed on him. That was commuted to seven years of transportation, but he offended again and this brought him a sentence of twice that period, at the other end of the world. But as he was waiting the move to a ship, the situation of hangman became vacant and he offered to carry out the work. He was eventually released in 1815, after serving as the city hangman for thirty-three years. Perhaps his most formidable challenge was the hanging of fourteen people in one day in 1813.

By the time Armley Gaol took over as the main site of executions for the county after 1864, a new breed of hangmen, such as James Berry and William Marwood, had emerged, but in York, another infamous figure was Nathaniel Howard. This man was involved in one of the most horrendous botched hangings ever carried out, that of Henry Dobson in 1853. *The York Herald* wrote that, 'The painful exhibition of last Saturday, when Dobson was executed, showed that, from old age and infirmity, [Howard] was totally incapable to perform the duties of his responsible situation.' Dobson took a long time to die, struggling violently on the end of the rope, with no swift method of hastening his end being able to be performed. In former times, with executions on the Knavesmire, it would have been possible for friends or relatives to pull on the legs of a hanged person struggling on the rope – hence the expression, 'hangers-on'.

Finally, there was Thomas Askern, a hangman with perhaps the worst drink problem of them all. Possibly his worst failure was in Durham, where the rope broke and the condemned man fell 15ft to the ground. Perhaps the most intriguing aspect of Askern's career was the hanging of William Dove, a most celebrated case from Leeds in 1856. Recent research by Owen Davies (*see* Bibliography) makes a good case for there being some uncertainty that Askern did indeed hang the celebrated wife-killer, and it is typical of the career of this true criminal 'character' that such a controversy happened in his lifetime.

In terms of the wider social history, a study of York Castle and the cases in its records, there is surely every variety of criminal in the chronicle. For instance, in 1809 *The Times* reported that, 'A lad named Brangate, 14 years of age, was last week committed to York Castle, charged by the verdict of a coroner's inquest with the murder of Catherine Furniss at Selby.' The boy did not hang, but could easily have done so. Other sad stories were the suicides – not a common occurrence, though that fact may be surprising to some. A typical case is that of a certain Riley in 1817. The coroner's inquest had been satisfied that he was deranged, and at York he had been watched carefully, but he still found a way to cut his throat. Reporters were always critical, of course, one writer commenting that '. . . we must doubt the propriety of confiding the custody of a maniac, who had already made one attempt upon his life, to his fellow prisoners.'

It has not been possible to include absolutely all of the prisoners executed at York. It would take several large volumes to accomplish that task. I have adopted the approach of including around 150 executions, covering the range of crimes from political to domestic and from sensational to representative. Some of the historical events related to the history of York executions caused a large degree of confusion and complexity: the Jacobite rising of 1745 is a case in point, and tracing the individual people who met their deaths at York (as opposed to other places) is virtually impossible. I have therefore included a group entry for that subject and others similar. The fundamental 'business' of the courts and gallows when it came to the condemned may be seen from these entries in the West Riding Sessions Papers (Doncaster) from 1637–8:

> John Saunderson of Epworth, Co. Lincoln, yeoman, for stealing on 23 Nov. 1637, at Wortley, a white mare, value 26s. 8d. the property of Richard Cressye, Witns. William Parkin, Pet. Particke, William Cressye. (Commited to York Castle and there found guilty and hanged by the neck.)

> Richard Hildierd of Horton, labourer, for stealing there on Dec. 1 1639 a stone and a half of wool, value 8s. the property of someone unknown. Wits. William Greene. (Committed to York Castle and there hanged.)

There are so many such cases on the record that the material we have amounts to no more than those few statements. On the other hand, many felons guilty of capital offences were not executed. In 1805, for instance, 350 people received a death sentence but only sixty-eight were hanged. After the loss of the American colonies in 1776, there was a period before Australia became a destination for transportation in 1788 in which one would have expected the number of hangings to rise, but statistics are scarce for that period. What is certain is that there was a very high proportion of transportation sentences in the years between roughly 1800 and the 1840s. In 1806, for example, 496 people at York received sentences of seven years' transportation and twenty-six had fourteen-year stretches.

The Castle Prison.
(Author's collection)

Barred windows at
York Castle Prison.
(Author's collection)

What follows, then, is a chronicle of the hangings mainly at York Castle but also at some of the other gallows locations in the city, over a period of around 600 years. From the centuries before 1700, I have included representative cases. However, I have included an appendix with a fuller list. Anyone seeking a comprehensive chronicle should look at the *Criminal Chronology* of William Knipe.

As a coda to the ongoing narrative of compiling these elusive records, I have to add that the Rowlandson picture of 'Mary Evans hanged at York 1799' appears to bear no relation to any actual hanging. Yet the image is surely one of the most illustrative of the horrendous scaffold scene at the core of these stories.

'Mary Evans hanged at York 1799' by Thomas Rowlandson. (York Art Gallery & Museums Trust)

1

HANGED & PARDONED

John Ellenstreng, 18 August 1280

Looking at the medieval period through modern eyes, it is hard to imagine the complex structures of authority of both the Crown and Church in all areas of an individual's life and death in a Catholic universe. The higher clergy had a high level of personal status and sway among their flock, and the wealth of the Church went along with this. Of course, they had their own courts as well, and their provinces were centres of great influence.

The old Ainsty area of York was integral to the Benedictine Priory at Micklegate, and the priory of Holy Trinity was a powerful establishment, with rights given to it by the King, reaching back to Henry I. One of those rights was the power over criminals who were apprehended within the Ainsty; this meant that such persons could be hanged in the area, and there was a Priory scaffold. King Stephen had granted land to the Priory, and as the gallows stood there, it was known for some time as 'the thieves' gallows'. This chronicle of hangings begins with what is arguably the strangest of all the tales, because in fact, the prisoner survived the hanging.

The man in question was John Ellenstreng. All we know about his offence is that he was 'convicted of larcenies' and so was sentenced to hang; he was a member of the Guild of the Hospital of St John of Jerusalem, and luckily for him, his fellow monks were allowed to take away the bodies of any of their number who had dangled from the scaffold. They came for him to give him a Christian burial, and when they arrived at their chapel (St James on the

Micklegate Bar, situated close to a gallows site, where the heads of traitors were hung. (Author's collection)

1

Castle Gate, a main thoroughfare used on execution days. (Author's collection)

Mount), to their amazement, John was still breathing. As was usually the case in the medieval centuries, myths were generated from this, maintaining that he had been saved by blessed intervention – that St James himself had saved John's life.

The man who had been 'hanged' on 18 August was given a pardon later by the King himself, after there had been a written account of the strange event by a witness, a man called John de Vallibus, who was one of the justices in the Eyre (circuit court) of York.

2

KING HENRY'S VENGEANCE

Robert Aske, 3 July 1537

During April and May 1537, Yorkshire landowner and rebel Robert Aske was in the Tower of London being interrogated about his part in what we now call the Pilgrimage of Grace. Henry VIII had pressurised and taxed the monasteries and other religious foundations across the land, and in 1536 this regime became intolerable to many people, particularly in Yorkshire and Lincolnshire. Aske had been one of the main leaders of that rebellion. Under pressure and torture, he said, among other things, that 'The abbeys are some of the beauties of this realm to all men and strangers passing through.' He was a man full of passionate causes and ideals.

Aske was also a man with a noble pedigree; his mother was the daughter of John, Lord Clifford. But when the rising came, he was happy to travel and communicate with everyone, often crossing the Humber to work with the Lincolnshire men, whose rising was focused on Louth. As the rebellion gathered momentum, Aske was on the march, carrying the flag of St Cuthbert. He and his men occupied York on 16 October 1536, and even the Archbishop of York joined them, taking their oath. Pontefract Castle was also captured.

Great numbers of nuns and monks had lost their livelihoods and status in the royal onslaught to plunder the wealth of the religious houses, and Aske insisted that these people be reinstated. Matters gradually escalated and there was a considerable level of military organisation; within months, towns across the north were garrisoned, and estimations of Aske's army are around the 40,000 mark.

Unfortunately, when his men confronted the Duke of Norfolk's force at Doncaster, wily diplomacy rather than force of arms defeated the rebels. Aske was persuaded to stop there, halt the rebellion and accept the King's pardon. He persuaded his followers to follow suit. It seems that the point had been made, and the threat was made tangible. Aske considered that to be enough. But he was dealing with one of the most brutal and repressive states in history with a body of treason law that was relentlessly applied to all and sundry.

The first sign of betrayal came when Henry began to make promises of reforms; a treaty was made, largely with the intention of stalling things so that the forces of the King could open another gambit. A second army went north with Norfolk at the head. Aske was called south with blandishments and lies and imprisoned after standing before a commission at Westminster. On 17 May, he was sentenced to death for high treason and then taken back north to York. He was ignominiously paraded across the land as he was escorted north, his destiny being the scaffold at York. Before he was hanged, Aske repented and also made it clear that he had been given a promise of a pardon but that it had been reneged. The most heart-rending story that persists from this event was that Aske's servant, Robert Wall, died of grief, so intense was the pain and suffering he went through, knowing that his master was going to be publicly hanged.

3

ALMOST AN ESCAPE

Thomas Wilson (alias Mountain), 30 July 1570

Thomas Wilson was charged with the murder of one George de Walton, the abbot of St Mary's. However, the abbot was just one of the victims of this man with two names, who entered the Church of St Peter's to wreak murderous havoc on 13 July 1570. Wilson also stabbed another clergyman, the Right Reverend Father in God, Edmund Grindall. It was to be a long trial, lasting four days, but the real drama came afterwards, in the gaol.

Wilson was found guilty and sentenced to die. He was put in the hell-hole of St Peter's prison to languish until the day of his death, but the man was wily enough to almost escape. He tried more than once to scrape and cut his way out, at one time using a piece of plate he had managed to shape into a cutting-tool. The desperate man made a hole through a brick partition and somehow managed to move into the gallery of the chapel, even with a weight of 50lbs in fetters strapped to his body.

The condemned man worked through a thinner partition and ended up under the roof of the building, but unfortunately for him, his movements were heard and he was recaptured. Wilson was eventually hanged at the gallows of the abbey of St Mary at Clifton.

4

A SUPPOSED WITCH

Jennet Preston, 29 July 1612

This is a case that smacks of corruption and skulduggery. Some historians have argued that Jennet Preston from Gisburn was hanged because she was the mistress of one Thomas Lister, and in being that woman, was hated by Lister's son. Before her trial that led to her death sentence, Jennet had been acquitted during the famous period of the 'Lancashire Witches' who had been tried at Lancaster. But after coming through that phase of crazed and irrational prosecution, she stood in the dock again in July 1612, accused of the murder of Thomas Lister.

Recent research on the case makes it clear that two powerful men, Roger Nowell (who had been High Sheriff of Lancashire) and Thomas Lister of Arnoldsbiggin, a manor house in Gisburn, Yorkshire, perceived witchcraft as a devilish, evil concept, not as something linked to the old ideas of the 'wise woman', a combination of quack healer and astronomer found in many communities throughout Britain for centuries. We have an account of the Preston story in a publication of 1613 entitled *The Arraingement and Trial of Jennet Preston of Gisbonre in Craven in the County of York* by Thomas Potts, who was a clerk to the court at York.

The ancient image of a witch, Mother Shipton, from an old print. (Author's collection)

Jennet was, according to Potts, 'maliciously prosecuted by Master Lister.' Her trial had been in relation to the death of Thomas Lister Senior, and young Thomas was convinced that Jennet had bewitched his father so much that he had died as a result. A servant had claimed that, as the older Thomas had died, he cried out 'in great extremity' that 'Preston's wife lays heavy upon me . . . help me, help me . . . ' Both the servant and young Lister had testified that the dying man had ranted and raved when he thought that Jennet was in the house, saying, 'Look about for her and lay hold of her . . . For God's sake shut the door.' They even said that after death, Jennet touched the corpse and blood flowed.

On top of that, Roger Nowell from Lancashire made more accusations; he claimed that Jennet, who had been married in Gisburn in 1587 and was thus much older than Lister when she was supposedly his mistress, had been well treated by the Lister family and had been seen in her true colours of 'witch' when the new master took over. The most damning supposed evidence was that Jennet was said to have gone to a gathering (a coven) of witches at a place called Malkin Tower. Nowell had allegedly investigated this and reported that Jennet and her peers had planned to 'put the said Master Thomas Lister of Westby to death, and after Master Lister should be taken away by witchcraft . . .'

But this all appears to be fabrication; historian Jonathan Lumby argues convincingly that Jennet was bullied by two powerful men. Potts wrote that she died on the scaffold 'impenitent and void of all fear or grace . . . she died an innocent woman because she would confess nothing.' The poor woman had been mercilessly victimised, the charges monopolising on the general fears about demonology and the Pendle Witches story. After all, even the King, James I, had written a book on the subject, and that volume, entitled *Demonologie*, was clearly very influential on general myths and fears.

5

A 'WICKED COURSE OF LUST'

Ralph Raynard & others, 28 July 1623

This scaffold story begins with the plain fact that a man named Fletcher married a woman from Thornton Bridge, and it was recorded that she had 'formerly been too kind' to a certain Ralph Raynard, an innkeeper from nearby Easingwold. The two kept up their secret liaison after the marriage, and as matters intensified, the moment came when the new husband stood in the way of their happiness, so they planned his death.

The conspirators approached a local roughneck named Mark Dunn from Huby, and a plan was conceived to take Fletcher's life; they lay in wait for him by a stream as he travelled from Huby. As Fletcher passed by, all three grabbed him and, after killing him, took the his body away to bury. The place they chose was Dawnay Bridge. Fletcher's wife had brought a sack for the body, such was her callousness; the three killers took the body and buried it in Raynard's garden, under a tree root, and sowed some mustard seed over the spot to cover it.

When people asked where Fletcher was, his wife replied that he had fled the law over a matter of some kind of civil writ; time went on and, as the first writer on the case wrote, the 'wicked course of lust' continued. But then things went wrong for the killers, springing from the fact that the dead man had long before that day suspected his wife of adultery and, even worse, because he wrote this rhyme which he sent to his sister, not long before he was murdered:

If I should be in missing or suddenly in wanting be,
Mark Ralph Raynard, Mark Dunn, and my own wife for me.

Some time later, as Raynard was stabling his horse en route for Topcliffe Fair, the story goes that the mead man's spirit appeared before him and told him to repent for the deed, as vengeance was at hand. The man became tormented and restless, and he was so much under duress, mumbling about the deed, that at last his own sister went to a magistrate, Sir William Sheffield, and told of the killing.

All three members of the murderous gang were arrested and went to York for trial. They were sentenced to die and were hanged at the Tyburn on 28 July, and their bodies were later hung in chains at the spot where they had killed Fletcher. Ever since, the place has been named Gibbet Hill. Raynard's home, where the victim had been buried, was not far away from the spot.

Execution by axe, an alternative to hanging. (New Popular Educator, 1890)

6

AN ASSORTMENT OF FELONIES

Eleven hanged, 1636–47

In the seventeenth century, executions were many and the crimes in question varied. There were so many capital offences that the hangmen were always busy, and the attitudes embodied in the criminal law statutes throughout the Stuart and Georgian periods testify to the 'zero tolerance' attitudes of the authorities. Basically, the situation centred around the general fear of damage to property and infringement of the game laws on the part of those who had land and property to defend and preserve. Opposed to them was, naturally, the mass of working-class people who had to feed their families and make a living in an atmosphere of severe repression and frequent privations, as they were at the mercy of economic forces beyond their control.

Indicative of this milieu is the case of Owen Thompson, a man from Snaith who was condemned for horse-stealing and hanged, along with Mary Harrison, who was just twenty-five-years old, at the St Leonard's gallows at Green Dykes near Walmgate Bar on 26 March 1636. Mary had poisoned Jacob Jackson on 5 January at Stockton, near the city. Similarly, Robert Skelton's crime was one very common in those years – that of forging a bill; he was from Hull, and he met his fate on the scaffold on 1 August 1639. His body was buried (not sent to the anatomists) in St George's churchyard, Bean Hill, close to Fishergate Postern.

Highwaymen and arsonists were, of course, much feared and these offences were rife in the late seventeenth century. A typical case of arson involved one John Taylor, a young man of twenty-one who set fire to a farm belonging to William Hodgson near Stamford Bridge on the night of 13 January 1641. He was hanged at the St Leonard's gallows on 23 April 1641.

There were many cases of highwaymen, not all famous, or infamous, as were the later figures of Turpin and Nevison. But certainly one much feared in his day was Amos Lawson, from Huddersfield. He had given Yorkshire travellers the terrors of a long and daring career on the road, making a good living from instilling fear into his victims. But in the Forest of Galtres on 3 April 1644, the sheriff of York captured him. This was William Taylor, and Lawson was out to rob him, such was his intrepid and foolhardy attitude to his criminal work. At Lawson's execution there was a large attendance; people out to enjoy the satisfaction of seeing the villain's dying struggles on the rope. The highwayman was hanged at the Tyburn outside Mickelgate Bar on 30 July 1644, his body was later buried at St George's churchyard.

Another case of highway robbery involved a whole gang who were caught and then hanged on 31 March 1646. Thomas Empson and four accomplices were executed at the Micklegate Tyburn for a robbery at Huddersfield on 10 February. On that day, Empson, along with John Dove, Joseph Dunning, Thomas Robinson and John Robinson went to their doom at the hands of the York hangman. There was a liberal attitude then to the disposal of their bodies, as these were given up to friends and relatives for burial.

On 10 April 1647, one of the most notorious poisoning cases at York was resolved with the hanging of two sisters. Elizabeth and Helen Drysdale were convicted of the murder of Robert Boss of Heslington and Robert Blanchard. A joiner and a woolcomber respectively, the men had been at the sisters' lodging house by the sign of the Maypole at Clifton on 16 February that year. The report of the trial states that the two young men were 'paying their addresses' to the sisters, and it seems that the poisoning had taken place over some time, without the men knowing what was happening to them.

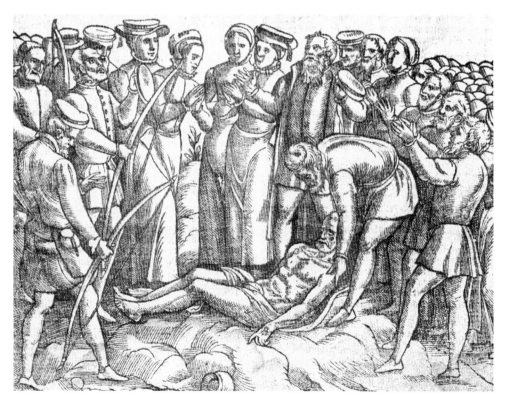

The burial of William Wiseman, showing how the burial of felons relied on friends' help. (Foxe's Book of Martyrs, *1880)*

St Leonard's Church, outside Walmgate, close to the former St Leonard's gallows.
(Author's collection)

7

A MURDER IN FULFORD

George & Maria Merrington, 13 April 1649

The Merringtons lived in Fulford, and their evil designs on William Rex of Dunnington came to fruition on 9 March 1649 when he came to their house for dinner. The couple grabbed Rex and strangled him with a length of cord. But seldom has there been such carelessness in a murder case as this. They buried him under the kitchen floor near the fireplace, but rather carelessly left a length of cord coming out from the floor.

Walmgate Bar, the final part of the route to the St Leonard's gallows. (Author's collection)

When a village constable came looking for the man who had disappeared without explanation, he found both the cord and the grave. From Constable Radge's arrest to the execution cart was a short period of time, and the day of their execution was an immensely popular day's entertainment for the populace.

When they were taken in the cart towards the St Leonard's gallows at Green Dykes, a huge crowd gathered and the sheriff's officers and a troop of dragoons escorted them. As they went down Castlegate, the cart could barely move for the mass of people packed into the narrow street. At the Pavement, sensibly, some people pushed back to force a route through for the cart. William Knipe, in his history of the case, wrote:

> In turning into Fossgate, the street was one mass of human beings. One woman had her leg broken in the crowd, and a young man had his thigh broken: both were removed by a doctor. On entering Walmgate, the same scene presented itself . . . The two culprits here fainted, and stopped before the house of Mr James Addindale, at the sign of the 'Golden Barrel'.

The sheriff let the condemned couple take some mint-water. It was twenty minutes past nine by the time they reached the scaffold.

8

FOURTEEN HANGED IN ONE DAY

Joseph Baines & others, 30 April 1649

On 5 January 1649, Isabella Billington, aged thirty-two, along with her father, crucified the wife and mother of a family at Pocklington. All we know is that a calf and a cock were offered in some kind of burnt sacrifice. It may have been a piece of 'magic' gone wrong, perhaps in an attempt to cure some horrible disease as in the famous case of Bridget Cleary in Victorian Ireland – or it may have been outright barbarism. Isabella and her father were two of fourteen people hanged on 30 April 1649. They were a batch of mixed offenders, some involved in rebellion and others merely everyday felons.

The hangman was busy and must have had assistants that day. First, there were twelve men, from Leeds to Bedale, all guilty of 'rebellion', and along with them was a mixed bunch, whose crimes give us an insight into the range of homicides fairly common at the time. There were several women: Hannah Meynell had tried to kill George Myers. We know she was 'a very stout woman' and that her body went to the surgeons. Ellen Nicholson had done one of the worst things possible at this place and time – her crime was incendiarism, as she had set fire to her master's house at Selby. She died, we are told, penitent.

All the culprits were dragged on sledges into Castlegate with a dragoon escort; when there were momentary pauses, all the condemned sang psalms together. When they reached the hangman, he was swift and merciful, sending all of them into eternity (if we believe the Victorian record) in 'about five minutes.' For that to have happened, there had to be a line of nooses in place and several assistants for the hangman. This was common practice, as with such later cases as the Luddites (see chapter 48).

9

SHEEP STEALERS HANGED

Leonard Gaskill & Peter Rook, 1 May 1676

The offence of sheep stealing was a serious crime for centuries, and of course in Yorkshire, where wool was the major industry in many parts of the county, it was dealt with severely. In one chronicle of crimes assembled in 1831, the author wrote: 'sheep stealers are generally found to be of the very lowest grade in society, desperate men whose fortunes are so low that they care not what they attempt to mar or mend them.' In later years, the penalty could often be a commutation from death to transportation, or as in one case from 1800, the death sentence was commuted to hard labour and a man was placed in the Wakefield House of Correction rather than hanged at York. But in 1676, two men were destined for the St Leonard gallows. In fact, they were the last two men to be hanged there. Leonard Gaskill and Peter Rook were from Beverley and their crime was very serious in the communal context of the town and its local commerce. The two men were very poor and pushed to commit a desperate act, a crime easily committed but also very speedily resolved, as farmers were vigilant and informers well paid.

Rook and Gaskill commemorated at a York inn. (Author's collection)

But Gaskill and Rook take a secondary place to the history of the St Leonard's gallows. They were the last people to be executed there, and in 1700, the Grand Jury at the York Assizes petitioned the judges for the removal of the St Leonard's scaffold. The Home Department at Westminister (the forerunner of the Home Office which was formed in 1782), gave permission for this, and on 3 June 1700, the gallows was no longer a part of the topography. After all, York had had far too many gallows for too long, so it is no surprise that the good citizens wanted to reduce the number of those disturbing reminders of the lowest behaviour of the criminal elements of mankind.

Gaskill and Rook would neither have known nor cared that their deaths have been remembered because they were a 'milestone' in the penal history of York. They were just one more statistic in a long line of criminals convicted for rural crime.

10

SWIFT NICK MEETS HIS DOOM

William Nevison, 4 May 1684

William Nevison is as much a mythic figure as Dick Turpin, and is perhaps Yorkshire's second most notorious highwayman. Most areas in Yorkshire like to claim him as their own, notably in the burgeoning heritage industry, but what is not widely known is that there is a strong oral tradition that he was active around Gomersal and Hartshead, and his most well-known deed there was a murder, when he shot the landlord of a public house near Batley.

Nevison's dark fame across the West Riding and South Yorkshire made him the subject of ballads and apocryphal tales; there is a cutting at Castleford called Nevison's Leap and an inn was given his name. The song 'Bold Nevison' has some patently untrue statements, such as:

> I have never robbed no man of tuppence
> And I've never done murder nor killed.
> Though guilty I've been all my lifetime,
> So gentlemen do as you please.

The main story of his life is supposedly the feat that won him the nickname 'Swift Nick': a ride north from Gad's Hill in Kent to York. He reputedly robbed a man in Kent and then made his escape on a bay mare, riding north at an incredibly fast pace, from Kent to York in a day.

We know that Nevison's father was a steward at Wortley Hall and that his brother was a schoolmaster, and we know that the robber himself was married and had a daughter. His wife lived to be 109 years old, dying in 1732. The oral tales pass on a complimentary view of Nevison, and a diary entry for 1727 records that 'at the same time there lived with this family Nevison, who afterwards was an exciseman, but being out of his place, became a highwayman.' This notes that he was with a family called Skelton who were Wortley gamekeepers. This detail makes sense, that an exciseman would find an attraction in the wealth attainable and turn tables to the wrong side of the law. Further investigation reveals that he started his criminal career when he began stealing at the age of fourteen. James Sharpe, in his book on Dick Turpin, says about Nevison: ' After being punished for stealing a silver spoon from his father, he stole £10 from his father and also his horse, and set off for London, cutting his horse and slitting its throat in case he be suspected . . .'

Sandal Church, where William Hardcastle is buried. (Old Yorkshire, 1887)

It is hard to believe that the robber who haunted the Leeds to Manchester road around what is now Hartshead and the northern fringe of Mirfield was also once in the service of the Duke of York and was at the siege of Dunkirk, but that is the tradition. Everything fits the description given to him in the Victorian period, when the myths were fully generated. One main piece of local tradition is that he used to visit one of his mistresses at Royd Nook and would visit an old inn called the King's Head north of Mirfield; he would most likely make his way from that base on to the Manchester road. The story goes that he stopped at an inn in Batley and the landlord recognised him. The man raised the alarm and came to tackle the robber, but Nevison shot him and rode away. Acccording to Victorian antiquarians, there was once a stone in a field near Howley Hall with the inscription: 'Here Nevison killed Fletcher, 1684.'

This was Nevison's last caper into the lawless valleys of West Yorkshire. He was pursued and finally tracked down and cornered at the Three Houses Inn at Sandal. He was taken to York and hanged. He was captured by William Hardcastle, who was buried at Sandal Church in 1696.

11

A LEEDS COUNTERFEITER

Arthur Mangey, 3 October 1696

In the *Annual Register* for 1832 is an account of what some workmen in Briggate, Leeds, discovered as they demolished an old house which had once belonged to a celebrated goldsmith, Arthur Mangey (sometimes recorded as Montjoy):

In taking down some houses . . . the workmen discovered in the roof a small room in which were found several implements used in coining, and a shilling of the date of 1567. The house in which they were found was occupied in the reign of William III by Mr Arthur Mangee [*sic*] a goldsmith who was convicted of high treason . . .

Before he fell foul of the law, Mangey was much respected; he had made the civic mace for the Corporation of Leeds and had been paid the sum of £60 for that in 1694. Mangey came from an old established York family who could trace their ancestry to a Freeman's Roll of 1555; he had relatives in York and the family were held in high esteem. But Arthur Mangey was to become the 'skeleton in the cupboard' of their family tree. In 1696 he was arrested for coining; this was the offence of clipping the coin of the realm in order to produce new coins from the clippings. He would be very skilled in that work, of course.

The tale is a classic one in the annals of crime – an accomplice told the law and that was the end of Mangey. He was tried at the York Assizes on 1 August 1696 and executed on 3 October. The reason for the long period of time between sentencing and hanging is that Mangey was reprieved twice. There are several manuscript copies of various accounts of his trial, which took place before Baron Turton. On one copy, signed 'John Shipley', part of the indictment is expressed in this way: '. . . for thou, not having the fear of God in thy heart, nor weighing the duty of allegiance to the King, but instigated by the Devil, treasonably, traitorously and against the known law of this land . . . did coin twenty pieces of money, of mixed metal, into shillings.'

Mangey pleaded not guilty. But his one time partner, George Norcross, gave King's evidence and doomed his partner, explaining to the court in detail how Mangey worked in the coining. Mangey fought back and the record states, 'in response, the prisoner endeavours to show that Norcross is an ignorant fellow'. But then one Dorothy Gervase entered the scene, testifying that she sold some clippings to Mangey. She and others then stated that they saw the attic room where the accused worked.

Things became clouded in court when it was revealed that Norcross was a bigamist. He had served some time in Rothwell Gaol, said a witness for the defence, while Mangey, on the other hand, was 'an honourable man'. But the judge, in his summing up, steered the jury towards a guilty decision and it took them thirty minutes to decide that the goldsmith was guilty. In those days this was, of course, a felonious crime, which meant that Mangey would forfeit his property, so in fact his family, and particularly his children, would lose their inheritance.

Two reprieves followed, but the judge would not act on them, so determined was he to see the man hang. Mangey was on the scaffold by 3 October, after having been ignominiously dragged on a hurdle to his place of death. Shipley's account describes what happened:

Standing under the gallows, he gave out and sung part of the 73rd psalm, from the 25th verse to the end, many persons joining in the singing. Then he addressed the onlookers, desiring them not to throw his ignominious death in the teeth of his wife and children . . . He then delivered a paper to the Sheriff, announcing himself ready to die.

The paper handed to the sheriff was a statement about the complicity of those who had testified against him. He was hanged at the Tyburn by Mickegate Bar. He never knew that, in fact, there were some proceedings taken against persons in Leeds, and one of these was Gervase, who had testified against him. She was fined. Perhaps the ultimate irony is that his name was still on the Leeds mace: 'Arthur Montjoy fecit'. But after a mayor in the Victorian period, Alderman Tatham, took office, the mace was re-gilt and the name removed.

In the account of Mangey's death given in a chronicle of York Castle, these lines are given with reference to his hanging:

Oh 'twas a fearsome sight to see
That pale, wan man's meek agony,
The glare of that wild, despairing eye
Now bent on the crowd, now turned to the sky . . .

12

DICK TURPIN

John Palmer (aka Dick Turpin), 7 April 1739

The name Dick Turpin has not only become the most famous (and infamous) criminal name associated with York, it has also become a name resonant with all kinds of myths and legends about the supposed highwaymen of the Georgian and Regency periods. Thanks to research by historians such as James Sharpe, we now know that the facts of the man's life are indeed far from the supposed facts of the popular narratives about him, disseminated in such works as broadsides, ballads, novels and poems. The strange tales of 'gentlemen highwaymen' could not be further from the truth. Most highwaymen were pathetic and incompetent, and certainly desperate and ruthless. Turpin was no exception. He may well be a feature of the busy heritage and tourist industries in the city, but we are now fully aware of the reality of his life and nefarious acts of cruelty and murder.

The basic facts are simple: He was born in 1705 and became an apprentice butcher; he began stealing and then joined a gang in Essex. He went into burglary as well, and when he was with the Gregory Gang in Essex, the outfit began to strike terror into areas of the county. He had started out as a man whose knowledge of butchery made him useful in cattle stealing, and then he progressed to some nasty criminal acts. With Gregory, the leader of the gang, he robbed a farmhouse and poured boiling water over the owner (an old man) and raped a woman there. His image in contemporary terms was rarely glamourised: he was once depicted in a woodcut throwing an old lady onto a fire. His first murder was of a man named Tom Morris, a servant who recognised him as a robber.

Matters stepped up a gear in terms of his infamy and sheer brutality when he joined Tom King, another highway robber; but it seems that Turpin killed his accomplice during a botched robbery. He then fled north. After that, he began to make a living from horse-stealing, and to do this, he stole horses in South Lincolnshire and took them up the Great North Road to sell in East Yorkshire. It was when the Yorkshire connection occurred that he assumed the name of John Palmer. But as with so many criminals, he was caught after a trivial piece of business. His first incarceration was in the Beverley House of Correction, and he was brought before magistrates in the Beverley Arms.

Palmer/Turpin was arrested for shooting a cockerel and the man involved in this incident was George Crowle, the man whose actions were to lead to Turpin being tried for murder at York. Crowle was the magistrate who was acting against 'Palmer' after he shot the cock belonging to Francis Hall in Brough (where Palmer had settled). Crowle was also MP for Hull and he made sure that the trial would take place in York, rather than in London. Of course, what had occurred to make everyone aware that Palmer was Turpin was that a letter had been intercepted and his handwriting was recognised. He faced charges of horse-stealing and murder.

James Smith and Edward Saward came from Essex to testify and Turpin was doomed. The judge asked if the accused knew any reason why the sentence of death should not be passed, and Turpin tried to come up with reasons to stay the trial. He even said, 'I am sure no man can say ill of me in Yorkshire.' But he was sentenced to hang and he took his last few steps in this world on the Knavesmire scaffold on 7 April 1739.

Even after death, though, his narrative continues with sensation and interest. His body was taken to the Blue Boar in Castlegate for public display, and then it was supposedly interred in St George's churchyard. But the doctors tried hard to obtain his body for dissection, as they

TRIAL

Of the Notorious Highwayman

Richard Turpin,

At *York* Affizes, on the 22d Day of *March*, 17͟3͟9, before the Hon. Sir WILLIAM CHAPPLE, Kt. Judge of Affize, and one of His Majefty's Juftices of the Court of *King's Bench*.

Taken down in Court by Mr. THOMAS KYLL, Profeffor of Short-Hand.

To which is prefix'd,

An exact Account of the faid *Turpin*, from his firft coming into *Yorkfhire*, to the Time of his being committed Prifoner to *York* Caftle; communicated by Mr. APPLETON of *Beverly*, Clerk of the Peace for the *Eaft-Riding* of the faid County.

With a Copy of a Letter which *Turpin* received from his Father, while under Sentence of Death.

To which is added,

His Behaviour at the Place of Execution, on *Saturday* the 7th of *April*, 1739. Together with the whole Confeffion he made to the Hangman at the Gallows; wherein he acknowledg'd himfelf guilty of the Facts for which he fuffer'd, own'd the Murder of Mr. *Thompfon*'s Servant on *Epping-Foreft*, and gave a particular Account of feveral Robberies which he had committed.

The FOURTH EDITION.
To which is prefix'd, A Large and Genuine Hiftory of the Life of TURPIN, from his Birth to his Execution; and of all his Tranfactions and Robberies, and the various Methods he took to conceal himfelf. The Whole grounded on well-attefted Facts, and communicated by Mr. *Richard Bayes*, at the *Green Man* on *Epping-Foreft*, and other Perfons of the County of *Effex*.

Y O R K:

Chapbook on Dick Turpin. (York Art Gallery & Museums Trust)

Dick Turpin shooting Tom King, from an old print. (Author's collection)

were always desperate for corpses to use in anatomy classes. The mob were aware that the medical men had this intention and a pamphlet of the time gives an account of the populace supposedly saving the body from the doctors. A certain Marmaduke Palms was bound over for trying to take the corpse for anatomy. In addition, men were charged with handling his body, as they acted to protect it from Palms, a surgeon.

Finally, although it is not certain, there is a grave that is supposed to hold Turpin's remains at St George's churchyard: a pathetic and possibly sham final resting-place of this notorious villain, whose mythology was perhaps confirmed when Harrison Ainsworth published his novel on Turpin and Black Bess, entitled *Rookwood* (1834).

13

DEWSBURY RIOTERS

24 July 1739

Riot and disorder are two words that run through the turbulent history of Britain, and often the cause of such terror in the streets is the rift between the 'haves' and the 'have-nots' in a

Right: *The Beverley Arms,
where Turpin first appeared
before a magistrate.* (Author's
collection)

Below: *Turpin's gravestone.*
(Author's collection)

hierarchical society. Throughout the eighteenth century in particular, riots could break out at any time, for a multiplicity of reasons. Sometimes the cause was the navy press-gang or the heavy-handed presence of the militia; at other times it could be a sense of injustice. Of all the reasons, perhaps the easiest to understand are the economic ones, because workers have always been at the mercy of the market-places and fluctuating retail and wholesale prices.

Such was the case in Dewsbury in 1739, but what was unusual about this large-scale and frightening mass disorder was that it became an occasion that was exploited by local religious factions, when the new Methodist movement in the Church of England was faced with many bitter enemies in the conservative ranks of the clergy. But these riots were bread riots – the price of flour had risen sharply and the citizens of the Dewsbury and Wakefield area went out into the streets and attacked the boulting mills where bran was sieved out to refine the flour.

In terms of legislation, the Riot Act of 1715 had been the formative statute, and it defined the threat exactly: 'A riot is an unlawful assembly which has begun to execute its common purpose by a breach of the peace and to the terror of the public.' Such offences in the eighteenth century were punishable by fines and imprisonment with hard labour, as they were seen as misdemeanours – not as serious as felonies. But it was not difficult to make discernible felony offences from the behaviour of the leaders of riots, and that is exactly what happened in this case, leading to four death sentences.

On 30 April, a massive crowd gathered in Wakefield, with the aim of stopping the 'badgers', or travelling salesmen, from making flour for export to other villages. There were soon around 500 people on the move, and against them, in an age long before there was any police force, was the High Sheriff of the county, Sir Samuel Armitage and Sir John Kaye. They took their servants along and tried to dissuade the mob from further trouble. But it was no use, and the mob merely stoned them. They then smashed a mill property at Thornhill and stole everything they wanted from the owner. As one report said at the time: 'The mob, supposed now to be of 1,000, came by beat and drum and colours carried before them in defiance of authority, but the gentlemen were not able to prevail upon them to return them to their homes.'

In the end, it was an act of extreme bravery that won the day for the authorities. The mob had destroyed a barn in Crigglestone and then threatened to take a man named Pollard and string him up 'and skin him like a cat'. But in stepped Captain Burton and boldly faced them. He knocked down two or three of them with his stick and then arrested half a dozen, taking them to the house of correction. After that, a detachment of soldiers arrived from York and the mob dispersed.

The Dewsbury men were tried at York on 22 July and four were sentenced to hang. Others were branded on the hand or transported for seven years. By 24 July, they were on the Knavesmire facing their deaths for that day of anarchy. They had been picked out as they were responsible for the violence and for the destruction of property, the latter being a felony and a capital offence.

The coda to the story, though, is that local churchmen tried to blame the trouble on a local preacher named Benjamin Ingham, a Methodist who had been educated at Oxford and had worked abroad with John Wesley. When he came back to his home town of Ossett, he started preaching and founding societies there. He was hated by such people as an anonymous writer to the *Weekly Miscellany* in 1740, who wrote: 'How much he [Ingham] may have contributed towards raising the mob I will not pretend to say, but what I am going to tell you of this clergyman is a matter of fact. I can prove it . . . A gentleman of Leeds . . . asked him what difference was there between the Church of England and his way of worship? To which Mr Ingham replied, "The Church of England is the scarlet whore. . ."'

It was all petty jealousy and squabbling, and mattered not one jot to the poor unfortunates on the scaffold.

A memorial to the Dacres, a border family caught up in the rebellion. (Author's collection)

14

YE JACOBITES BY NAME

Twenty-three rebels hanged, October–November 1746

After the defeat of the Jacobites, who had risen in support of the Young Pretender, Bonnie Prince Charlie, and who were thoroughly defeated on Culloden Moor on 16 April 1746, the trials of the prisoners were inevitable, and of course they were, as we now use the term, 'show trials.' Britain had plenty of people still alive who could recall the last Jacobite rebellion, in 1715, when the Old Pretender came south, but he had failed as well.

Most of the first trials of rebels took place in London, so Newgate was busy, but as time wore on trials were held across the north. There were both trials and executions in Cumberland and in Yorkshire, with twenty-three men being hanged at York. In the north-west, nineteen were hanged at Carlisle, seven at Penrith and seven at Brampton. As John Prebble has pointed out in his book, *Culloden*, one of the few good things to come from that miserable year was the ballad, *Loch Lomond*, referring to the journey home of one of the bodies, moved back over the border.

In York, a series of trials was inaugurated with a solemn service on 2 October at which the chaplain of the High Sheriff officiated. His quote from the Book of Numbers would have given no comfort to the men down in the cells awaiting their terrible fate: 'And the Lord said unto Moses, take all the heads of the people and hang them up before the Lord against the sun, that the fierce anger of the Lord may be turned away from Israel. . .'

The judges had seventy-five men before them and seventy of them received the death sentence, but it took something special to save the lucky five at the first sittings, who instead were handed down prison sentences. The most well-known example in the Jacobite records is that of John Ballantyne, who was acquitted because he had witnesses who stated that he had been dragged from his bed and pressed into service. As one witness stated, 'They did not even allow him time to put on his clothes . . . and they placed a guard on him . . .' Ballantyne's neck was saved and he threw his bonnet into the air in joy, shouting, 'My Lords and Gentlemen I thank you. Not Guilty!'

Twenty-three of the seventy were hanged and the rest were either transported or saved by joining the English Army – and many did the latter, of course, in order to fight another day, but not for the Stuarts. But twenty-three were hanged, and that dour procession of doomed men began their last walks in early November. Their crime was treason, so they were hanged, and then drawn and quartered, unlike murderers, whose bodies would usually be given to the surgeons. The hangman had the distasteful task of holding up chunks of body parts and saying to the mob, 'Behold the four quarters of a traitor!'

Of the line of men walking to the noose, one stands out for special mention: the piper, James Reid, who was the last man to hang, on 15 November. Reid's attempt at defence had been that as a piper, he was a non-combatant. The man from Angus, who had served in a regiment led by Lord Ogilvy, stood and awaited his fate as his counsel argued that he was not a soldier but a musician. But it was of no use. Chief Baron Parker, who had led the Exchequer and Common Pleas, and was a man of immense importance and authority, stated that, in that context and indeed in all, Reid was as much a soldier as anyone else. He said, '. . . a Highland regiment never marched without a piper, and therefore his bagpipe, in the eyes of the law, is an instrument of war.'

Reid's friends and peers who died just before him are remembered only in the statistics and muster rolls of the fates of Jacobites in that ill-fated enterprise against the Hanoverian dynasty.

In the main record of the executions, the reader is assured that, 'The whole of the proceedings was conducted throughout with the utmost decency and good order. Two hearses were ready to receive the bodies of Captain Hamilton, Clavering and Gordon, and coffins for the rest. The heads of Conolly and Mayne were set up at Micklegate Bar, and the head of Hamilton was put into a box, in order to be sent to Carlisle . . . '

15

THE MASS POISONER

William Smith, 14 August 1753

Of all the chronicles of criminals in the library of crime and law through history, arguably the most successful and notorious is *The Newgate Calendar*, first published in 1775, and then added to over the next fifty years. By the 1820s, they had expanded even more, and to be included in this series of narratives of foul deeds was a kind of twisted glamour and notoriety for a villain. The Yorkshire cases in the work are few, but one notable York execution that figures in the calendar is the tale of William Smith.

Smith was a farmer at Great Broughton; he liked land and a comfortable lifestyle. In fact, he liked it so much that, when his widowed mother married a second time, to a certain Thomas Harper, Smith was not happy about it. Even worse, Harper had two children who came along with the deal, and Smith saw much of his inheritance receding. He decided that he had to find a way to get rid of the old man and his children. The first attempts were legal – efforts were made to try and exclude them from his mother's will – but when this failed, more desperate measures entered his head. The story goes that he was at an apothecary's buying medicine for his horses when he concocted the notion of using some arsenic on his enemies. He was a man of good social standing and well respected, so the apothecary sold him two-pennyworth of the poison. At that time, there were no controls in the retail of such poisons as arsenic, and as this substance had a number of domestic applications, it would have been in common use.

On Good Friday 1753, some hot-cross buns (known then as 'Good Friday cakes') were made especially for the family, which was to be Smith's occasion for dropping the poison into the mix. He mixed the arsenic with the flour. It was only a matter of sheer good fortune that some of the neighbours did not come along for that particular meal.

William Harper and his children ate some cakes and all three of the intended victims died. Smith's nerve failed him and he knew that the finger of suspicion would point his way. He ran away to Liverpool, while his victims were slowly dying in intense pain. But this is a story of inner torment: Smith, unsure what his next course of action might be, could do nothing but return home – whether through guilt or remorse, we will never know.

It was a simple matter to have Smith arrested and detained, and soon he was standing at the Autumn Assizes before the judge, Mr Serjeant Eyre. Not only did the apothecary stand witness, along with a servant who had seen William with the poison, but Smith himself eventually confessed to the crime. He was hanged on 14 August at the Knavesmire.

THE

TRIAL,

Conviction, Condemnation,

Confession and Execution

OF

WILLIAM SMITH,

For Poisoning his Father-in-law,

Thomas Harper, and *William* and *Anne Harper* his Children,

At *Ingleby-Manor,* in *Yorkshire,* by mixing Arsenick in a *Good-Friday* Cake, who was tried on *Monday* the 13th of *August,* at the Assizes held at the *Castle* at *York,*

BEFORE

Mr. Serjeant *EYRE,*

And Executed on *Wednesday* the 15th, and afterwards dissected by the Surgeons of that Place.

To which is added,

An Account of the Murder of Farmer *Harvey,* his Wife, Son and Daughter in the Parish of *Brent,* within Sixteen Miles of *Plymouth,* who were found murdered on *Friday* the 10th of this Month.

L O N D O N:

Printed for M. Cooper, *Pater-noster-row,* W. Reeve, *Fleet-street;* and C. Sympson, at the *Bible-warehouse, Chancery-lane.* MDCCLIII.

Chapbook on William Smith. (York Art Gallery & Museums Trust)

16

THE SCHOOLMASTER KILLER?

Eugene Aram, 6 August 1759

The story of schoolmaster Eugene Aram and a mysterious death in Knaresborough is arguably Yorkshire's most mysterious unsolved case of murder. This may seem a strange thing to say, given that Aram was sentenced for the murder of Daniel Clarke and subsequently hanged; but the truth is that there are several doubts surrounding Aram's guilt. It is tempting to suggest that enemies wanted him charged and out of the way; after all, a former friend gave evidence against him, even though the evidence clearly made the man, Houseman, an accessory.

Aram was born in Netherdale in 1704 and he was something of a prodigy of self-education. His father was a gardener, but Aram was clearly destined for a career in the field of learning and education; he spent some time in London as a bookkeeper and then came home to Knaresborough in 1734, where he gained some experience as a tutor. Later he became a schoolmaster and moved to Lynn in Norfolk. We are asked to believe that a learned gentleman with a good income would mix with characters of disreputable character, because a murder was committed some time within the period between Aram being employed in Knaresborough in 1734 and the finding of a body in 1758. In that year, a labourer digging ground to make a lime-kiln at Thistle Hill found a human skeleton. At the coroner's inquest, someone stated that fourteen years before, a man named Daniel Clarke had disappeared without a trace. The names of Aram and Houseman were linked to Clarke, as they had been friendly at the time.

Eugene Aram. (Notable British Trials, 1913)

This is where the drama of this case begins: Aram was traced to Lynn and arrested, then brought back to Yorkshire for trial. He stood trial at the York Assizes. But all writing about the alleged murder since has focused on some crucially important questions such as who was the body? There was no proof it was Clarke's. Also, the testimony of Houseman, who was the main witness called against Aram at York, was clearly biased and untrustworthy. In addition, so-called evidence was all circumstantial. But perhaps most remarkable of all was the fact that Aram conducted his own defence.

At that time (and until 1896) the accused could not speak except in response to the judge's call for 'anything to say' at the end, before sentence was passed. Aram acted for himself and did a thoroughly efficient job of it. The narrative that emerged is one that suggests Aram, Clarke and Houseman were often together; that Aram's marriage had been a failure and his wife had become an implacable enemy against her former husband. These factors became part of the tale of guilt put together by Houseman. He claimed that the three men had exploited the fact that Clarke had 'come into money' when he married; valuables were gathered on credit, based on his wife's income (so Houseman said). Then the thieves fell out, and Houseman claimed that on a February evening he had seen Aram batter Clarke to death in a field as they walked in front of him. Aram rightly argued that Houseman would not have been behind them but walking with them, to an important meeting, and also that on a dark February evening he could not have seen such a thing. Another important detail was that Aram had had a very serious illness at that time, leaving his face scarred and his whole constitution weakened.

The most persuasive reasoning in Aram's own defence covered such things as his lack of a motive in committng such an awful deed, and that his basic character and temperament did not fit well with such a murderous act. Aram said of himself:

> Could such a person in this condition take anything into his head so unlikely, so extravagant? I, past the vigour of my age, feeble and valetudinary, with non inducement to engage, no ability to accomplish, no weapon wherewith to perpetrate such a fact; without interest, without power, without motive, without means . . .

He also destroyed whatever medical and forensic details might have been deduced from the found skeleton. He sensibly said that it could have been anyone, from any time. But all this was of no use. Judge Noel was impressed, but there was no material change in attitudes. Aram was thrown upon the mercy of the court and the jury found him guilty.

In gaol at York, he attempted suicide, trying to cut his arm with a razor; yet we have, as Lord Birkenhead pointed out long ago, a mystery in that a second letter alleging to be by Aram was found, and it was one that had clearly been fabricated by someone. We do know that Aram wrote some last words and also a poem. He said 'Though I am now stained by malevolence and suffer by prejudice, I hope to rise fair and unblemished. My life was not polluted, my morals irreproachable, and my opinions orthodox.'

Eugene Aram was hanged at York on 6 August in a most pathetic state, mainly through the loss of blood he had suffered; his wrists were bound and bloodstained. The ultimate insult to this man, who may have been a killer but who had never had any solid evidence set against him, was that his body was suspended in chains in Knaresborough forest – a kind of gibbeting meant to deter other potential malefactors.

An interesting coda to this story is that in 1837 a woman living in an almshouse at Wisbech told a writer for *The Gentleman's Magazine* that she had been a girl when Aram was arrested at Lynn and she saw him at the time. She said that the boys of the school had been in tears at the arrest, so much was Aram esteemed by them. The most interesting note from her memory was that she said Aram turned bodily when looking behind him – never merely turning his head. The writer in 1890 who recorded this, added, 'Has any poet, any observer of nature, ever depicted this instance of fear mustering up resolution?' The writer, R.V. Taylor, appears to be trying to suggest that Aram exhibited some kind of possible guilt and fear. As with everything connected with this tragic tale, the truth will never be out.

THE
GENUINE ACCOUNT,
OF THE
TRIAL,
OF
EUGENE ARAM;
For the MURDER of
DANIEL CLARK,
Late of *Knaresbrough*, in the County of YORK;

Who was convicted at YORK Affizes, *August* 3,
1759, before the Honourable WILLIAM NOEL,
Efq; one of His Majefty's Juftices of the Court
of *Common Pleas*,

To which, after a fhort Narration of the Fact, is perfixed,

An Account of the remarkable Difcovery of the Human
Skeleton at St. ROBERT's CAVE, where it had lain up-
wards of Thirteen Years.—A Detail of all the Judical
Proceedings, from the Time of the Bones being found,
to the Commitment of RICHARD HOUSEMAN, EU-
GENE ARAM, and HENRY TERRY, to *York Caftle*.—
The Depofitions of ANNA ARAM, PHILIP COATES,
JOHN YATES, &c.—The Examination and Confeffi-
on, of RICHARD HOUSEMAN.—The apprehending of
EUGENE ARAM, at *Lynn*, in *Norfolk* :——With his Ex-
amination and Commitment. ——To which are added,

The remarkable Defence he made on his Trial:—His own Account of himfelf, written after his Condemnation :——With
the Apology, which he left in his Cell, for the Attempt he
made on his own Life.

All taken immediately from the Original DEPOSITIONS,
PAPERS, &c.

The FOURTH EDITION.

YORK:
Printed for C. ETHERINGTON, Bookfeller, in
the *Pavement.* M.DCC.LXVII.

Aram's poem has some of the most stoical and impressive lines ever written from the
death cell:

> Calm and compose, my soul her journey takes,
> No guilt that troubles, and no heart that aches.
> Adieu thou Sun; all bright like her arise;
> Adieu fair friends, and all that's good and wise.

A THEFT IN THE MARKET PLACE

Isaac Turner, 6 March 1766

The slender information we have about Isaac Turner and the two unfortunates who were hanged with him in 1766 tells us more about the criminal justice system of the time than about the nature of thieving and larceny. Roberts and Lambert were two linen drapers in Sheffield at the time, and Isaac Turner stole some goods from them. He was hanged with two other burglars, Thomas Taylor and Abel Hobson.

The mid-Georgian period was the heyday of the application of the 'Black Acts' – the extreme measures brought in after the 1720s and added to as the number of capital crimes increased. The most fortunate person in Turner's case was Lydia Nicholson, who was charged with receiving the goods stolen by Turner: she was acquitted.

It is difficult to find statistics on crimes for the year in question here, but around the turn of the eighteenth century, the crime figures for burglary, in terms of numbers sentenced and then executed, are indicated as in the following example: between 1814 and 1820, 1,765 were

The flogging yard at a penitentiary, part of the harsh regime at this time. (Author's collection)

sentenced and only 111 were actually hanged. The tendency was to transport most; Turner was unlucky, and so were the two burglars. Turner had committed grand larceny, as the goods he stole from a dwelling house were valuable; but still the figures were on his side: in the same years as before, 892 were sentenced for that crime and only twenty were executed.

Turner was tried before Mr Justice Bathurst, which may have been the reason why the three were sentenced to hang that day – a hard, straight judgement with no leeway; or it may have been that he had had no powerful friends, a detail that seems to be highly likely. Turner, Taylor and Hobson stepped out onto the scaffold on the Knavesmire on 6 March.

18

CRIME OF PASSION

Thomas Aikney, 20 March 1775

The tale of Thomas Aikney is inextricably linked to that of Elizabeth Broadingham, as the latter was an accessory to murder. As Thomas actually killed Elizabeth's husband, John, he was guilty of murder; whereas the wife was found guilty of petit treason. A wife found guilty of murdering her husband would have to be burned at the stake, and the best a woman convicted of that crime could hope for would be to have someone strangle her before the flames got to her. Much later than this, in the early years of the next century, there were campaigns in parliament to change the law and stop this barbarous practice, but in 1775 that was the sad lot of a number of women.

Unusually, this case was not the more usual one of a woman administering poison. Elizabeth was having a good time with a younger man, Thomas Aikney, while John Broadingham was in prison. It is not clear why she wanted more than the affair with its excitement, but she did, and in fact she persuaded Thomas to kill her husband. It appears that Elizabeth was wily enough to pretend to return to normal family life when John returned home, but all the time she was still in discussion with Thomas to do the desperate deed and to free her from her marriage. Thomas argued that the best course was for them to elope and start a new life elsewhere, but in the end Elizabeth won and Thomas was pushed into an attack. He waited at the door of the house as Elizabeth told her husband that there was knocking downstairs. He rose from his bed and went down, and as he opened the door, he was stabbed in the body and thigh.

Thomas ran off, leaving the knife still sticking in John's stomach; the report of the incident says that John staggered out into the street and called for help. People found him 'holding the bloody knife in one hand and the other supporting his bowels, which were dropping to the ground.' He died the following day, and both Thomas and Elizabeth were charged and arrested. Thomas was hanged and his body given to the surgeons for dissection, while Elizabeth was led through the streets on a hurdle to her place of death. There, she was strangled as she was tied to the stake, and then the fire was lit. The usual disgusting scenes followed, at which people gathered her ashes as macabre mementos of a now notorious criminal.

Death was swift for both Thomas and Elizabeth, but she had had the accompanying terrors and humiliation that the rituals of burning entailed.

19

WHITBY MEN ON THE GALLOWS

Thomas Lawrence, William Fisher & others, 1772–1796

In the last decades of the eighteenth century, lawlessness around Whitby led to some dramatic and brutal tales. There were six such notable crimes whose perpetrators ended on the Knavesmire. Most typical was perhaps the highway robber, Thomas Lawrence, who robbed a certain William Knaggs of Whitby, taking 30s from him. He was also a military deserter, so the local reports said, and he was hanged on 21 March 1772.

Another robber from the fishing port was William Fisher, who broke into the house of Thomas Walker and stole money to the value of £5. He was hanged on 15 March 1773. Two years later, John Williamson met his fate on the York gallows for robbing the Whitby mail at Thornton Gate. He took over £66 from the coach. In 1787 William Bryan was hanged for stealing 4s 6d, four farthings and some clothes from a weaver at Common Dale named John Ricardy. He died on 1 April that year. In terms of items stolen, the theft of a mare was always going to result in either a hanging or a life sentence in Van Dieman's land (an old name for Tasmania), and in 1787 Timothy O'Brien did just that, taking a dark bay mare from a man named Robert Duck at Lyth. He was hanged on 7 April that year.

There was also a violent man in this period, one James Rice, who was dangerous with a knife as well as with his fists. He stabbed to death Thomas Westill, a sailor from Staithes, after an argument at Hinderwell. Rice was hanged outside Micklegate Bar.

St Margaret's Church, where many paupers in York were buried. (Author's collection)

Finally, we have a desperately nasty tale of the robbery and assault of a York Jew named Innocenti Rossi by Thomas Maclean and two accomplices, as he was travelling by Stone Haggs. They robbed him of £2 4s 6d. The victim was a pedlar, and would hardly have had much wealth. Perhaps his only valuable possession was a silver watch, and the Maclean gang found and stole that as well. It was recorded of Maclean that he was 'quite a lad' – but that reputation only added to the weight of opinion against him that led to his hanging on 25 April 1796.

20

A ROBBERY IN ATTERCLIFFE

John Vickers, 30 March 1776

John Vickers, a true renegade and worry to all good people, was born in Hemsworth back moor, but went on the rampage around his own area in Sheffield around midnight on 11 February 1775. He was out to steal and take away everything he could, however small. First he joined up with a man called John Booth and they stole money (including a bad shilling), along with mutton and half a pound of butter from John Murfin, whose home was near the Blue Ball public house.

Vickers was clearly the leading light in a fairly large band of villains around the area, and he wasn't satisfied with the first nocturnal foray into the homes of peaceful citizens. He went out again, this time with three other men, and his target was anyone who might happen to come out of the local hostelries the worse for drink. But his luck ran out, because one of the intended victims was a man who knew Vickers. He was in fact a former employer in the days when Vickers had been an apprentice. Before that, Vickers and his gang had also robbed John Staniforth of money, mutton, sugar and flax. Again, they located a spot near a public house to attack – this time the Glass House.

Now that the law had his name, Vickers was soon tracked down. He was soon at York, along with Booth, facing two indictments in front of a grand jury. The facts of his robberies on both Murfin and Staniforth were then ascertained. Booth was acquitted, but Vickers had the death sentence passed on him. Mr Justice Gould put on the black cap and spoke the terrible words with the phrase 'hanged by the neck' in the familiar few sentences. Vickers was indeed hanged, at the Tyburn on 30 March 1776.

21

THE KIRK EDGE KILLER

Frank Fearne, 23 July 1782

Apprentice file-smith Frank Fearne was a man many locals thought would never be worth anything; today we might call him a waster. But he stepped up from simply being a man with a bad reputation to become a murderer when he focused on Nathan Andrews as his victim. Fearne was born in Bradfield, and was a man with a head full of dark and dangerous plans and plots. The plan that led to the murder began in 1782 when he called on Andrews' shop in Bradfield to tell him all about a watch club he had said he was putting together. Andrews clearly saw this as a good retail opportunity and agreed to go with Fearne to meet the members.

Of course, Fearne had other ideas. He returned to the shop on the arranged day armed with a gun and a knife. On 18 March, they walked to Fearne's village, the watchmaker having been spun a yarn about the club having around twenty members: this would make his walk and time away from the workshop seem worthwhile.

But as they walked along at Kirk Edge, they passed someone who knew Fearne and this was to be his downfall. A man named Wood nodded hello and Fearne answered. That brief encounter would lodge in Andrews' mind, of course. A little later on the walk, Fearne let Andrews walk in front of him and then callously shot him in the back. After that, the man's violence against his victim was horrendous: he knifed Andrews and then clubbed him with a hedge-stake.

Fearne stole some watches and ran off. Wood later returned to the spot and found the corpse of the watchmaker. He ran to raise the alarm and bring help. Several local people came to the scene of the crime. The only problem, after the body had been carried to the nearest workhouse, was that no one knew the dead man's identity. But gradually, it dawned on Wood that he was the man he had seen walking with Fearne earlier that day. Naturally, friends and family were wondering, as time went on, where Andrews was. The general alarm led to action by the magistrate and the hunt was on for Fearne as he was the only suspect.

A constable went to find him at Hawley Croft, where it was known he was staying in some lodgings. Taken from his bed, he was arrested and taken into custody. The stolen watches were soon discovered and there was no doubt that Fearne was the killer. He was destined for the York Assizes. There he faced Mr Justice Eyre at the Summer Assizes. Fearne's confidence that, without witnesses, he would be set free, was ill-founded. The jury found him guilty of murder. Not only was he sentenced to hang, but his body was to be gibbeted as well, such was the heartless violence exhibited in his act of cruel murder.

The judge did not let the body go for dissection but ordered the gibbet to be placed on Loxley Common. Fearne and three others were hanged on 23 July 1782. Writer David Bentley has recounted the tale that, at the gallows, Fearne took off his shoes and threw them into the expectant crowd waiting for the spectacle of his death. He said, 'My master often said I would die with my boots on so I have pulled them off to make him a liar!' It was observed that he 'died hard', and later the body was carted away to be gibbeted, where it rotted. It is on record that his skeleton fell down from the gibbet in December 1797, on Christmas Day.

22

A PAIR OF BURGLARS

William Sharp & William Bamford, 19 August 1786

This brief tale is indicative of the many hangings at York about which the biographical details are sparse indeed. We know that these two men broke into a house belonging to Duncan McDonald, a button-maker from Sheffield, and that they took some horn combs and just 7d in cash. For that offence, paltry as it seems, they were both sentenced to hang. They were tried at York and hanged at the Tyburn on 19 August 1786. All we know in addition to this is that Sharp was from Conisbrough and was just twenty-six years old, and Bamford, just two years older, was from Rotherham.

The case illustrates not only the occasional application of the full power and terror of the law when the 'Black Acts' were in operation, but also the sheer number of practically anonymous people who felt the noose around their necks after an horrific ordeal from trial to death cell. The most harrowing aspect of these cases is that the punishments were seen by many as merely routine and perfunctory.

23

THE ROBBER
BUTTON-MAKERS

John Stevens & Thomas Lastley, 17 April 1790

This is the strangest and most baffling account of a process towards a death sentence that has surely ever been recorded. It began with nothing more than a prank brought about by a group of workmates who had taken too much beer. But in March 1790, a large and irate crowd gathered on Lady's Bridge, Sheffield, calling for the blood of a button-maker, John Wharton. Just days before, news had arrived of the trial of four men in Wharton's trade; men whom he knew well and who drank with him. Three of the men had been sentenced to death, and it had all been over the 'theft' of a basket of food from the market.

It all began with a drinking session at the White Hart in Waingate. It was a Saturday night in August and Wharton was drinking with his mates in the basement. He had told his wife that he would not be home late and he stood up, stating his intention to leave, saying, 'I'm off home.' It was the beginning of the kind of friendly prank that has been going on among workmates for centuries, but this one went badly wrong. Wharton went to the lavatory and left his basket of food outside. The other men, who had followed him, trying to persuade him to stay, decided that they would take the basket. They went on to another inn, the Barrel in Pincher, Croft Lane, and there they asked the landlady to cook some of the mutton that was in the basket.

By that time, Wharton had made his way home, but en route he met Constable Eyre and complained to him of the theft. It seems that Eyre assured Wharton that he would teach the men a lesson for that, and he went to the Barrel to check that they were there. He heard the noise inside and went away, meaning to return later. When he did go back, all was quiet but there was Wharton's basket in a cupboard. Eyre, much to his discredit, knowing the seriousness of the resultant consequences, went to a magistrate to sort out an arrest of the men. There were four men involved: John Stevens, John Booth, Thomas Lastley and Michael Bingham. The constable got hold of warrants for their arrest.

It is unclear at that point what the real intentions of Eyre were. If it was a partly humorous move, to worry the men and have a laugh at their expense, then the obtaining of actual warrants does not fit with that. He must have known that such warrants could possibly lead to more than an appearance before a magistrate and a fine or a warning. Indeed the worst did happen: the men were arrested. Stevens was taken to the Town Hall and put in a cell; the others were tracked down one by one, as word was circulated that they were being searched for by the law.

Before magistrates, evidence was taken about what the men had done and why. They all corroborated the tale that the whole affair was a joke, but they were remanded in custody. At the second hearing, the contents of the basket were itemised: a shoulder of mutton, a pound of tobacco, half a stone of soap, £7 of butter and 4*d* in cash. Technically, the 'joke' was indeed a felony. They were committed to York Castle.

Mr Justice Buller at the York Assizes was, in many ways, at a distance from the local context. How could he possibly understand the male behaviour of suck a prank among workmates? As for Wharton, he had taken offence and could see no fun in the business at all. The jury found Stevens, Lastley and Bingham guilty of the felony and they were sentenced to death. Booth was discharged, as witnesses had sworn that he was merely a bystander.

The crowd which gathered at Lady's Bridge were shouting Wharton's name and were ready for revenge. Both Wharton and his wife fled for their lives as their little shop was broken into and smashed. The premises were then set on fire, and nothing was heard of them after that.

The question was: would the men actually hang? Surely there would be a reprieve, it was thought. The course of action decided on was the most extreme action possible: a petition to be presented to King George III. In four days, some representatives from Sheffield took a coach to London with a petition in their hands. There they did indeed obtain a reprieve. But the real drama was still to come. At that time, the Great North Road was the only route

The Assize Court.
(Author's collection)

for all efficient travel north, and it had become flooded around Lincoln. A messenger was sent to York with notice of the reprieves, but he arrived too late to save Stevens and Lastley. Fate smiled kindly on Bingham: his reprieve was not needed. For some reason, the judge had commuted his sentence to transportation for life.

So, for a public house prank, when men were in their cups and wanton, two men had been hanged. Obviously, the case was a local sensation, and one local poet wrote these lines, which sum up the fiasco:

> We took John Wharton's basket and meat
> But not with an intent to keep;
> Like Judas he did us betray;
> For money he swore our lives away.

24

BARE-KNUCKLE FIGHTER HANGS

George Moore, 17 April 1790

The button-makers were joined on the scaffold that day by George Moore, a bare-knuckle fighter. He was a blade-forger from Sheffield Park and a local celebrity, having fought many times at Crookes Moor, one of his most famous struggles being with a tough scrapper named Dewsnap. Moore had had a chequered career, and had enlisted in the army, joining the 19th Foot in Sheffield. But when the regiment was billeted in York, he and some friends engaged in a robbery.

Moore and the others broke into a hardware shop in York owned by William Davis. They stole a few things and were not difficult to trace, being dressed in their uniforms. Moore was convicted and sentenced to death. He was moved to write a farewell poem, as Eugene Aram had done, penning lines from the death cell:

> I, George Moore, must tell you plain,
> I lose my life for little gain;
> For shopbreaking that shameful deed,
> It makes my tender heart to bleed;
> A harlot's company I did keep,
> To think of her that makes me weep;
> Through her I took to evil ways,
> Which is the short'ning of my days...

He stood on the scaffold with the three button-makers at the Tyburn. Perhaps the saddest footnote of all these stories belongs to Moore, because there is an account of his father setting out from Sheffield to see him in his last hours, but the old man stopped for a drink on the way and drank so much that he had no money to pay for further travel. He turned for home, saying that he could do his son no good, anyway.

25

ARSON ON A MAGISTRATE'S HOUSE

John Bennet, 6 September 1791

This is a crime story very much of its time: it happened as a result of a move to enclose the common land of Crookes Moor, where working men could spend their small leisure time profitably and freely. The area of land in question was vast – 6,000 acres. An Act of Parliament had been gained by some powerful landowners who had land in the Moor, men such as the Duke of Norfolk and the clergyman Wilkinson. The workers were furious, and not long before that, there had been major riots in Birmingham, eventually put down by the militia.

On 13 July 1791, when the commissioners arrived to enclose the land, they were confronted by some local die-hard workers who terrified them with threats. As usual, in affairs of public disorder, men in the wealthier classes asked for help from London, some writing to the newly-established Home Office, demanding militia. The request was acceded to, and some dragoons from Nottingham arrived.

There was a massive crowd in the streets when the dragoons arrived; riots were commonplace for all kinds of reasons. In this instance, the occasion was used to free a man who had been arrested for debt, which boosted the crowd's morale. But the powder-keg was lit when the officer who had arrested the debtor insisted on getting his man. When he was retaken, the officer, one Schofield, was effectively under siege from the crowd. The riot spread to other centres of resentment, such as the house of Vicar Wilkinson, a magistrate. He lived at Broom Hall, and the mob went with the intention to burn the place down. As some men were inside, other went out into the enclosed garth to burn four haystacks; a servant there saw what happened.

People arrived to help put out the fires, and the mob moved on to attack other property, including that of the constable, Eyre. By morning, more soldiers had arrived, and the land and property involved was retaken, and, of course, arrests were made. Foremost of the arrested men were John Bennet, who was only eighteen, and three or four others, some of whom had merely been in the wrong place at the wrong time. Bennet and a man named Ellis were charged with riot and arson and committed to York for trial.

These types of crime were taken very seriously; they were the easiest methods by which the poor or those with grievances could wreak havoc and fear in the ranks of the wealthy, landed classes. Four men were in the dock, Bennet among them, as the trials began. A familiar event occurred: someone turned King's evidence. Ellis testified that Bennet had been the main offender when the stacks were set alight. Other witnesses were called, and we have to suspect that these were paid 'yes men'; all a part of the process to ensure that someone would swing for such a terrifying offence.

Bennet was young, and he was also an apprentice with some years still to serve under his master. But supportive statements mattered not one jot: Bennet would have to be seen to be punished severely for such an offence and he received sentence of death from Baron Thompson. John Bennet was hanged with another arsonist and a forger on 6 September. Another man, Johnson, had been luckier. He was acquitted due to the fact that, as one witness said, he 'was ever considered weak in the head and easily persuaded.'

The local men of power, who had been hated and had been the targets of the crowd's anger, appear to have deserved much of the poor opinion. Vicar Wilkinson, for instance, was recorded as having put a little girl in the stocks for repeating a scurrilous verse about him:

They burnt his books
and scared his rooks
and set his stacks on fire.

Meanwhile, just in case the rabble were outraged again, the city had its own barracks established in 1794, with accommodation for 200 men.

26

THE ROTHERHAM HIGHWAYMAN

Spence Broughton, 14 April 1792

Spence Broughton could have been a successful farmer, had he stayed on the right side of the law. Broughton had a farm bought for him at Marton, near Sleaford, when he was just twenty-two. He also gathered more wealth when he married a woman who brought money with her, but all this was not enough for this bad seed, a man who was, in the words of his time, a rake and a villain. He began by gambling, and he mixed with bad company, including a certain John Oxley.

With Oxley, contact started with a London fence named Shaw, and soon Broughton and his friend were taking on robberies. They were paid to rob the Rotherham mail, and the two men got to Chesterfield, from where they would begin the attack. Not far from Rotherham, the two men stopped the coach. There was only the post-boy driving; he was tied up and left. The robbers took the bag but there was little worth having – merely a bill of exchange, though that was for a large sum.

While Broughton stayed in Mansfield, Oxley went to London with the bill. His problem was to convert it into money. In London, with the help of Shaw who had set up the job, Oxley saw that it was possible to do the business and walk out with the cash, in this case from a company in Austin Friars. After giving Broughton just £10 initially, Oxley found himself at the point of being pressured for more, and it seems that Broughton was pleased to take another £40.

Of course, now that the two men had come across a simple means of stealing funds, they were out on the road again; they robbed the Cambridge mail this time. Their difficulties began when a provincial bank note was traced – one of a number the two men had been working hard to spend in order not to be traced. But they were traced, after the energetic and sharp activities of a shop-boy. Some Bow Street officers traced the lodgings where Broughton was staying and, after a chase, they cornered him at an inn called the Dog and Duck. Broughton was taken to Bow Street. Their London contact, Shaw, turned King's evidence and told the whole story of the robbery at Cambridge, and of where and how they had dealt with and hidden the takings.

Later, the two men were examined again, and although the post-boy could not identify them, they were remanded in custody. The enterprising and wily Oxley managed to escape

An old woodcut of a highwayman, an inspirational image from an old print. (Author's collection)

from Clerkenwell Bridewell; he disappeared into the night and we know nothing more of him. But Broughton was taken north to York. He was tried before Mr Justice Buller at the Spring Assizes in 1792. There, Shaw gave evidence against him again, and also against a man named Close who had assisted in the financial transactions in London. Broughton was told by the judge that there was not 'a shadow of hope' of any mercy.

Spence Broughton was to be hanged, and also gibbeted. He was reported as having faced the sentence with fortitude, and he prepared himself for death, and was reportedly what the authorities would have called 'a model prisoner'. He died with four others on 14 April 1792, and before he died, said, 'This is the happiest day that I have experienced for some time.'

The story of Broughton does not end there, however. His body was gibbeted on Attercliffe Common, not far from the Arrow Inn and there was a weekend, like a local feast day, with his body being pulleyed up into position on the Monday morning. But some years later, in 1827, a man named Sorby bought the land around the gibbet, and a few years before that, when some of the bones of the highwayman had loosened and fallen, the tale is told of a local potter who took some of the skeleton's fingers and used them to make bone china items. One of these, a jug, was sold in London in 1871. Such is the notoriety of this Sheffield rogue that over the years people have horded and preserved anything related to his story, and in one of the York archive stores, a piece of the gibbet has been preserved.

27

RIOT & DESTRUCTION

Will Atkinson, 12 April 1793

Will Atkinson has to be one of the oldest people hanged at York. He was a mariner, and well-respected in his home town. What is most heart-rending about this tale is that he and his accomplices had acted in a way they considered just. They had attacked and destroyed a house in Whitby in which the hated members of the press-gang used to meet and stay. The press-gang was simply one of the many forms of legalised violence in that turbulent time, along with whippings, extortion, enclosure and brandings. Periodically, the hatred and resentment would spill over into public disorder, and Atkinson was caught up in such a riot.

He and others were charged with aiding, abetting and counselling a number of rioters whom had completely destroyed the house, owned by John Cooper. Atkinson insisted that he had merely been present when the riot took place, but he was not believed. A writer in the *Whitby Repository* of 1868 recalled that the execution was well remembered 'by many persons forty years ago who were then living.' The oral history recounted depicts the old man encouraging the rioters, saying, 'Well done my lads, if I was as young as you, I would soon make the highest stone the lowest!' He was recalled as being 'good-tempered' and we might conjecture that his prominent and vocal presence at the riot was noticed by those in authority, and, as a result, he became a marked man who would have to be seen to be punished.

28

A CASE OF BESTIALITY

John Hoyland, 9 August 1793

The crime of bestiality is hardly the most prominent in the chronicles of British crime, and there is precious little literature in the records. The foundation legislation may be traced to a statute of Henry VIII in 1533 which makes no distinction between buggery with any creature: 'buggery committed with mankind or beast' was a hanging offence. Trials for buggery became more frequent in the eighteenth century, and even as late as 1822 a man was hanged in Ilchester for buggery with a sow. Sentences were severe, and as late as 1884 there was a case in Lincoln in which a teenager was given ten years' penal servitude for an unnatural offence with a ewe.

Cases in the York records are rare, but the pathetic instance of an old man from Attercliffe was an offence that led to the noose. This man was John Hoyland, and he was seventy-seven years old when he was charged and convicted of bestiality. Hoyland, it seems, was regularly beaten up by his sons and was altogether a sad and weak individual. The records state that at times he was 'frequently weeks together with bruises upon him.'

Two men accused Hoyland of bestiality; they claimed that they had seen him buggering an ass. Many locals thought that the two men had simply picked on the weakest person they could find to accuse, in order that they might obtain what was known as 'blood money' – sums given for the declaration of certain crimes, encouraging entrapment or the use of the law for vindictive purposes. The rewards given in some cases could be as high as £40, so it was an inducement to tell lies. Unfortunately, the case went from the magistrates' court to York, and there the jury believed the accusation.

Old John Hoyland was hanged on 9 August at the Tyburn, protesting his innocence.

29

MURDER IN THE NURSERY

James Beaumont, 18 July 1796

Despite the title, this story has nothing to do with children, or with plants. The nursery in question is an area of the Wicker district in Sheffield which was the Nursery of the Duke of Norfolk. From the Nursery area came filesmith James Beaumont, a man living apart from his wife, with another woman. On 9 May 1796, Beaumont strangled his partner, Sarah Turton. He had clearly had some kind of mental storm and was in a murderous rage; he went from Sarah to his wife, who lived in the area known as Barley-field; his aim to strangle her as well.

His wife, seeing that he looked highly unbalanced and was obviously out of all control, did not let him onto the premises. It did not take long for the hue and cry to catch up with him and Beaumont was caught and charged. Before long he was committed to York Castle and was tried at the assizes in the summer.

It was a plain, direct case: he was a murderer and Mr Justice Lawrence sentenced him to death. Surprisingly, his wife visited him in the condemned cell. We have no record of any account of possible insanity, nor of an appeal. The man merely said that if he had listened to his wife he would not have been in that position. The records show that his wife lived well after his death; but as for Beaumont himself, he was hanged on 18 July at the Tyburn.

30

THE MOTHER-IN-LAW MURDER

Ann Scalberd, 12 August 1794

It took Mary Scalberd six days to die. She had been bed-ridden and had suffered horrific agonies on each of those days, insisting all the time that her daughter-in-law, Ann, had poisoned her. Was this true? The only way to find out was to bring in the best medical men available. Mary had been attended to by George Swinton, a Dewsbury surgeon who heard the woman making the accusations. No detail in this report hints at why this might have happened. How it was done is no mystery: arsenic was used around the home at the time for all kinds of purposes, mainly as a pesticide, as most homes had a problem with vermin. It was easily available and almost anyone could buy a quantity from a druggist as these retailers were not regulated until after the 1851 Arsenic Act.

Arsenic does not make for an easy death; when the most typical form, white oxide, was used, it caused a burning sensation in the victim's throat, followed by violent vomiting. The skin then becomes bluish in hue before the final collapse. The experienced doctors who attended Mrs Scalberd would have seen this familiar pattern of symptoms. Before an inquest was held, because of the suspicions aroused in Swinton's mind, a well-respected doctor named Benjamin Sykes was called in to help. He was a graduate of the highly-regarded Guy's Hospital (founded in 1724). Sykes, who was near at hand in Gomersal, joined Swinton at the post-mortem. Sure enough, they both agreed that Mrs Scalberd had died of arsenical poisoning.

Mary's long and painful death was now fully explained, and Ann was responsible. Mary Scalberd's death had been caused by a steady administering of arsenic, and as medical expertise pinpointed the cause, so the finger pointed at Ann, who was tried and convicted. She was hanged on 12 August 1794.

31

MURDER OF A BASTARD

Mary Thorpe, 17 March 1800

At York in 1800, twenty-two-year-old Mary Thorpe pleaded not guilty to the charge of 'murdering her male infant'. It was the first capital offence tried in Yorkshire in the new century. One of the very first accounts of the case, published in 1831, keeps back much of the material around the story, simply pointing out that Mary began domestic service at fourteen, was happy, and then was seduced 'by one, whilst he pretended to lead the confiding girl on to happiness, brought her to ruin, misery and disgrace.' It appears that there was no knowledge of the identity of this man.

This course of seduction and ruin is arguably the typology of the infanticide chronicle throughout centuries of English history. In Mary Thorpe's case, the facts are chillingly simple: a woman friend helped in the birth of the child, and then a week later, Mary took the child to a pond and threw it into the water, a stone tied around its neck. This account seems too vague; Mary in fact stayed with a widow named Hartley in Sheffield for the delivery, than said she was moving on to Derby to be with her sister. But her plan was to go to Ecclesfield. It was there, in the river near Bridge Houses, that the child was thrown into the water, tape tied tightly around its neck.

The child had been strangled before it was thrown into the river, and there was no doubt that the tape around its neck was Mary's. Hartley identified the material. There was, of course, an inquest following the discovery of the little body. The charge was murder, and the coroner arranged for Mary to stand trail at York. The opinion of one commentator at the time was simple but powerful: 'The wretched girl became a miserable mother, and gave birth to a child whose smiles became her reproach.' The defence was that Mary had been delirious and not aware of what she was doing. The surgeons agreed that Mary had been suffering from 'milk fever' but that this was not sufficient cause of any palpable insanity.

AN EXECUTION AT TYBURN, YORK, 1799.

An execution at Tyburn. (From The History of York Castle, *1898)*

When the sentence was passed, Mary 'bore it with great firmness and curtseyed very lowly to the court before she left it.' She was hanged at the York Tyburn on 17 March.

32

TRIPLE HANGING

Sarah Bailey, John McWilliams & William Dalrymple, 12 April 1800

John McWilliams was careless. He did not keep himself organised and in control. He was also fond of forging the King's currency, and these two features together were a recipe for disaster. In his case, his doom was certain the night he left a bundle of banknotes in a public house in Sheffield. He had gone to that place looking for a room, but they had had none. When he left, he forgot to take his notes with him and a servant found them. It was well known that there had been forgeries around and a constable was called.

McWilliams was traced to another hotel where he had found a room for the night, and when the law arrived, he was found with more notes on him, these having been forged from one plate, using the format of a local bank. He also had two watches on him, bought recently and paid for with the forged notes. He had had no defence and was soon before the magistrates charged with 'uttering' bank notes, and, while the local constable had been busy following McWilliams's footsteps in his criminal activity, they had traced an accomplice, a Doncaster butcher. The man had panicked and had destroyed some forged notes after being tempted to pass some by an offer from McWilliams of 7s for each note passed.

The jury did not even have to leave their box at York before a guilty decision was given. Mr Justice Rook passed the death sentence, and McWilliams was hanged along with two other unfortunates: Sarah Bayley, who had also forged notes, and William Dalrymple, a bank robber. All three left this world at the Tyburn on 12 April 1800.

The York Gallows. (Illustrated London News, 1850)

33

THE LAST HANGING ON
THE KNAVESMIRE

Edward Hughes, 29 August 1801

By the end of the eighteenth century, pressure was growing among the more enlightened classes (and the race-goers) to end the hangings on the Knavesmire. For many decades, the days for racing had been planned to match hangings, so there were dual attractions for the mob. People from the more cultured and refined establishments complained about the repulsive sight of crowds baying for blood and entertainment at the scaffold. The *York Herald* summed up the situation in April 1800:

> The plan some time ago recommended by Major Topham for altering the place of execution for this city, is, we understand, now likely to be adopted . . . it cannot be otherwise than desirable that the public business of the city, the feeling of the humane, and the entrance of the town should no longer be annoyed by dragging criminals through the streets.

The man who has gone down in history as the last victim of the hangman on the three-legged mare is Edward Hughes, who was a soldier sentenced to die for committing rape. His victim had been one Mary Brown of Tollerton, near Easingwold. Hughes was only twenty, a Roman

Catholic who was serving in the 18th Dragoons. His response to the death sentence was a delivery of one of the most rhetorical statements made by a condemned man at York.

Hughes was Irish, and he made it clear to the judge that he was begging for some sympathy, and indeed for a commutation of the sentence: 'I assure your Lordship that the state of inebriety I was in on the day on which this unfortunate circumstance took place, was such as to deprive me of any recollection of the business, and if your Lordship's mercy should extend so far as to mitigate the punishment . . . I may hereafter become a useful member of society.' The young man even made the point that there had been no rape, but simply an attempt at rape, and played the last desperate card of referring to a witness who had not been called: 'There is also a woman . . . who lives in the house with the girl and her father, who will come forward and certify upon oath that the girl hath not received the least injury from the attempt at rape . . .'

Hughes had everything we might expect at a defence case, including character references from senior officers, but it all came too late at the conclusion of the trial, because of course he was unable to speak earlier in the proceedings, and clearly had no fit and competent counsel working for him. His words were all to no purpose. Edward Hughes was hanged, the last patron of the 'Mare', on 29 August 1901.

34

DOMESTIC TRAGEDY

Martha Chapel, 16 June 1802

Martha, sometimes called Mary, Chapel, was just nineteen and in domestic service with Colonel Surtees of Ackland when she faced the judge and jury at York on a charge of infanticide: a similar predicament to that of Mary Thorpe (see chapter 31). Chapel's story is, however, unlike that of Thorpe in one important respect – that she and the father of her baby were in love, and only parted because of the exigencies of hard times.

Martha courted a young man who was also in service, but as a contemporary account puts it: 'The young man to whom we have alluded became careless of his duties, excited reprehension and resolved at length, in that tumultuous year 1801, to take refuge in the army.' The sequence of events that led to Martha's downfall is the material of much literary tragedy. She and the young man walked out together and went to a local feast; her man had begged her to take some time off work. They had a good time, and of course, it was a rare opportunity for them to make love. Sure enough, that one fateful union led to her pregnancy, and in the way of grand opera, her young man left for the wars and was never heard of again.

In June 1802 Martha gave birth to a baby girl. There appears to be a strange aspect to the story of the birth, as recounted in the trial report, where it is stated that Miss Surtees, the Colonel's daughter, called for a doctor on the day Martha went into labour. Somehow, for months, the pregnancy was concealed from the master's family. Poor Martha was warned of the dangers of 'destroying children' when in such a state of despair. But the actual birth is the focus of attention as we try to understand the events. It seems that she had had a terrifyingly painful birth, and as one report says: 'Some time after, cries were heard . . . Half an hour after, blood was seen on the bed; and on search, a new-born female infant, dreadfully lacerated, was found between the bed and the mattress of an adjoining bed, its mouth was torn down to the throat, and its jawbone forced away . . .'

A Victorian illustration of a woman on the gallows. (Illustrated Police News, 1866)

A Pontefract surgeon witnessed this and appeared in court to verify the medical condition of the child. He considered that there was some explanation, bearing in mind the girl's distraught state. Through modern eyes, we understand the potential delirium and even hallucination that attends such stressful experience, but back then it was virtually impossible for 'temporary insanity' to be shown. The jury were asked to consider the possibility that Martha, out of her wits, had attacked the child and then hidden the corpse. Her statement in defence was that she had never meant to harm the baby. She said, 'I cannot recollect how or where I did it; if I did, God knows I loved the child before I saw it.' She said again, 'I am a wretched woman. It was my child. I never meant it any harm.'

Fittingly, the judge, a man seasoned to face this kind of lamentable situation, pronounced the sentence with some expression of emotion after Martha had been found guilty of murder. A few days later she was hanged. She was so mentally tough that she even endured a wait as there was a problem with the knotting of the rope. One writer reported that she '. . . died without a struggle, amid the audible sobs of the multitude.'

35

BRUTAL MURDER OF A WOMAN AT HOME

John Terry & Joseph Heald, 3 March 1803

This is a murder case in which the killer was so clumsy that he was caught within hours. Elizabeth Smith lived in Flaminshaw, Wakefield, in 1803. She was sixty-seven and well liked. She was self-sufficient; something quite rare at that time for a person of her age. She was also very enterprising, and her main source of income was her small dairying concern; she kept a few cows, and when two of them died, she was in trouble. Fortunately, she had a son in Leeds who was wealthy enough to finance her until she was back on her feet.

The downside of close communities is that most people know everyone else's business, and it was known around the area that Elizabeth had received cash from her son, and that it was obviously in her house. John Terry and Joseph Heald, two men of doubtful reputation, set about putting together a plan to steal this money. It would be an easy matter to rob an old lady on her own. But they were clumsy burglars and Elizabeth was awake when they entered her home; she came to investigate the noise and surprised them. She was brutally kicked and battered, and then Terry took a razor and slit her throat.

Everyone in Flaminshaw knew the two malefactors and they were soon detained and taken to trial. It was simply a case of 'thieves fall out' after that, and neither had a defence of any kind. It took a last-minute rant on the verge of the gallows for the probable truth to emerge. Terry put on a performance for the crowd, jumping up and down and haranguing them. But just before he was grabbed and pinioned, he said that he had killed the woman and if they hanged Heald, they were hanging an innocent man.

Perhaps in a modern court the likelihood would be that Heald would be considered an accessory, but things were simpler then: two men were in a room where an old lady was murdered, so it was 'natural' to hang them both.

36

A PARRICIDE CASE

Benjamin Oldroyd, 27 May 1804

Of all the varieties of homicide, the murder of a parent must rank high in terms of sheer public moral revulsion. In nineteenth-century Yorkshire, there are a few instances which stand out, and the woeful tale of the Oldroyd family is arguably the most heart-rending. The son who took his father's life was most likely mentally unbalanced, as he was suffering from cancer, a variety which was causing him to bleed from the neck. But nevertheless, he brutally killed his father in a most shocking way, and, in 1804, there was little toleration for alleged temporary insanity.

Benjamin Oldroyd was born in 1757 near Wakefield, where his father, Joseph, kept a small farm. According to a writer of the 1830s, the boy was always stubborn and of weak intellect. It appears that he was over-indulged by his parents and he never really had any schooling. He was 'confirmed in evil habits' and fell in with some rogues. As time passed, he became more and more wild and unrestrained, out of all control.

As he reached manhood, he was utterly full of hatred and contempt for his father. Joseph tried to impose discipline when it was much too late, and after that he tried morality and strictures; to the son, this was oppression. They constantly fought, and the enmity increased; when Benjamin developed cancer things became much worse. Then, on 18 July 1803, as Joseph said he felt ill and lay down on a bed kept in the parlour, Benjamin, now a grown man of over forty, raging in pain, grabbed his father and tied a rope around his neck, and then dragged him up higher so that he could be hanged from a hook. There Joseph struggled, kicking his legs and fighting for life, as his son watched.

After the old man had died, Benjamin waited for his mother to return home. The attack had taken place at noon, but it was six hours before mother and son raised the alarm. During that time they dragged Jospeh's body outside and fastened it to a cherry tree, to make it appear as if he had committed suicide. Of course, the coroner's court was not convinced, and basic forensics revealed the obvious facts that there were no rope-marks on the tree and also several bruise marks on the back of the man's neck which told the tale of a struggle before being suspended from the tree.

Mrs Oldroyd claimed that father and son had never quarrelled, but she said of Benjamin, 'When his bleeding fits come on, my son is like a madman.' She said he often seized his father 'with dreadful imprecations' and she had been afraid that one day he would murder Joseph. All the evidence pointed to murder, and the coroner committed Oldroyd to York Castle. There he appeared before Sir Allan Chambre, a man who was later to be lenient with Luddites in the north-west and gained a reputation for humanity; but in this case, everything pointed to Benjamin having the intention to kill his father and of carrying it out on the fateful day. The surgeon, Mr Thomas, said that death was caused by strangulation and added, 'The rupture of the carotid artery might proceed from the deceased having committed suicide, but I do not think it probable that anyone in that case would have composure enough to place the rope, with the exactness necessary, to produce this effect.'

Oldroyd was found guilty and the sentence of death was passed. But as it was clear that Oldroyd was deaf, of a weak intellect and also suffering from cancer; twelve judges conferred on the case and so there was a short respite. The report on him in gaol was that he behaved 'with perfect apathy, not to say insanity.' On 20 May the sentence of death was confirmed; after that Oldroyd became a handful and fought everyone, up to his last moments on the scaffold, when he refused to join in the prayer and shouted, 'It's wilful murder to hang an innocent man!' He fought and struggled with the officers until he fell flat on his face. As the noose was placed around his neck, he still screamed and fought. But on 27 May 1804, Benjamin Oldroyd became one more criminal statistic at York Castle.

37

'A PROFLIGATE CHARACTER ACROSS YORKSHIRE'

Joseph Waller, 16 March 1804

About four miles from York, as he was travelling homewards, Thomas Potts made the mistake of letting bystanders know that he was carrying money. He had had a bet over a trifle with the landlord of the inn where he had stopped, and in the room was Joseph Waller. Waller followed Potts on the road and befriended him; they stopped at one more place and as dusk came on, Waller pounced.

The attacker fell behind Potts and then hit him with a stick. As he was down on the ground, Waller struck his victim on the forehead, almost knocking him unconscious. The haul from the robbery was two five-guinea notes, and for that he had almost killed his victim. He went back to the inn where he had stopped with Potts and tried to change one of the notes, one from a Hull bank. He paid for a drink with coins and then left. When it came to the alarm being raised and the attack being described, the hunt was soon on for Waller.

The robber was eventually found by a constable near Wetherby at an old turnpike house, behind a bed, covered in sacking. At York, there was no trouble in identifying him and he had no defence; Judge Chambre passed the death sentence and Joseph Waller was hanged, the only one of a bunch of robbers who was not reprieved at that time. Chambre said that Waller was 'A profligate character across Yorkshire.' It was noted that Waller 'exhibited a brutal insensibility to his situation, and made no confession.'

38

ANOTHER INFANTICIDE

Ann Heywood, 18 March 1805

Ann Heywood was born in 1782, the daughter of ordinary working people. She had had no proper education and it appears that there was no real moral guidance or parenting in her background. As with so many others, her destiny was to go into service. What was remarked, though, by writers at the time, was that she had moods. She was reportedly of a violent nature and it was noted that 'Her temper had, more than once, deprived her of situations.'

The former York police patrol base, Walmgate. (Author's collection)

This statement implies that she drifted from job to job, losing her place and then having to work hard to win back her reputation. But all this comes to nothing in the face of what happened to her: she was courted, and then dropped and abandoned. In April 1804, she found that she was pregnant. The father had backed out of a promise to stick by her. She moved on and found work in Rotherham, working for a family named Roodhouse. She managed to hide the fact that she was with child and carried on her duties. Incredibly, she went on with her daily routine until she reached a point very near to giving birth.

The tale told at her trial was that she came downstairs to work on 30 November, and then began to go into labour. She went to a building outside the main home to have her child while another servant covered for her. This was surely the behaviour of a woman with amazing strength. But an allegation was made soon after that she had murdered the newborn child. In court it was said that she had stabbed the child many times and then stashed the body out of sight in an outhouse. She was apparently sent to stay with someone in Mosborough and while she was away, the little body was found. She denied the murder and said that she had been in a distressed state at the birth and had no real knowledge of her actions.

At the Spring Assizes Ann stood in the dock at York, facing a murder charge. She pleaded not guilty; it was obvious to writers at the time that she was a sick woman. Mrs Roodhouse stated that Ann had been ill during the period up to the killing but that she had continued working. 'She complained of much cold in her limbs' she said. Then the full story of the day of the birth emerged. Ann had been found staggering around in the kitchen. When they searched for her later, she was found in the outhouse. The maid said that 'her hands were covered in blood.' After a search, a penknife was found under her bed, and two days later the body of the baby girl was found, covered in cuts and slashes.

In the death cell, Ann confessed to the crime and in her desperation, she repeatedly asked for the father of the child to be brought to her. Typical of those hard times, though, she had to share the scaffold with John Wilkinson (see chapter 39) and they prayed together. The crowd was not as boisterous as usual and a writer noted that 'the number of females in the crowd was very great.' When the drop fell, it was noted that 'she expired without a struggle.'

The condemned cell at York Castle. (Author's collection)

39

HE POISONED HANNAH

John Wilkinson, 18 March 1805

It was said of John Wilkinson that 'The religion . . . was mere outward sign; with the word of God in his mouth, he harboured fiendish designs in his heart.' He planned the murder of his wife for a period of years, as he was known to be a restless spirit, a man who needed the company of what were then described as 'women of disreputable character'. Domestic life became strained, and his wife, Hannah, a good and virtuous woman, began to fear him. His apparent spiritual experience which took place in 1802 did little to change his daily habits and his basic temperament.

Wilkinson decided that his wife stood in the way of his life of dissolute pleasure, and she would have to go. He bought some poison and placed it in her food; she went out to work to support the family and he had her deadly meal waiting for her when she came home. When she retuned to work after eating, she fell violently ill and died. The inquest on her body made it clear that she had been killed by means of white mercury and the finger pointed at her husband as the primary suspect. Witnesses were found, such as the druggist who had sold him the poison; the suspect had asked if rats were fond of fish, as he was having a problem with rats. The druggist had said that they were, and Wilkinson had taken the mercury.

Mr Teale, the surgeon who examined the body, testified to the presence of the poison, and a witness named Ann Sporton said that two months before Mrs Wilkinson's death, she had complained of a burning in her throat and had said, 'Oh, what has the rogue been doing with my dumplings!' She had been given some oil to make her vomit on that occasion. The statement written by the accused and given to the jury certainly did not help matters. He claimed that his wife had been a nervous, jealous, suspicious woman and that she had

A York pub marking the city's macabre history. (Author's collection)

continually accused him of trying to poison her. He said that he had joked at times, after she had thrown food away, pretending he really had poisoned the food.

Baron Graham passed the death sentence and said, 'Far be it from me to embitter the remaining moments of your existence by dwelling on the enormity of your crime, except as I wish to produce in your mind those sentiments of conviction and sincere repentance which may be acceptable to the throne of grace.' Wilkinson, before he was removed from court, said that he had no fear about his soul.

When asked in the death cell about his guilt he simply said, 'That is best known to myself.' On the scaffold, with Ann Heywood (see chapter 38), he prayed aloud, and the ordinary (the gaoler) said that he must pray for Ann as well, a fellow sufferer. Wilkinson stopped and then said, 'Lord, save *us* . . . '

40

'A FEAR HAS COME OVER ME'

John Robinson, 8 August 1807

Susannah Wilson had been in the service of young farmer, John Robinson. She became pregnant by him and left his employment. But not long before she went to an arranged meeting with him, she told her cousin, 'A fear has come over me, and if aught ill happens to me, look to nobody but Robinson.' She went missing and a search was made for her; she had last been seen alive on 16 February, and her body was found on 27 March, near a sledge road that Robinson had made. Her body was well preserved, and the foetus of a female child was found in her womb.

Naturally, Robinson was charged with her murder. Elizabeth Green related to the court her cousin's words and her fears about the man. William Terry, who had been working for Robinson, then said that his master came in on the evening on which Susannah had gone missing, and had told him that he had to go to Staithes to collect some money owed to him. Later, in March, Robinson told Terry to cut some thorns so that a sledge road could be made on the land, and this entailed filling ditches. When the witness was asked what use could be made of this road, he answered, 'No use at all'. When asked about the road, Robinson said that Terry had helped him dig it, when, in fact, he had simply cut the thorns. When the servant had asked him about that, the accused had said, 'You must say so, or they will say I murdered the girl.'

Various people reported on the fact that Robinson had been getting drunk and reports confirmed that he was losing control as suspicions arose about him, and then another man testified that the sledge road could not have been made without the digger seeing the body of the dead woman. The surgeon reported that Susannah's skull had been fractured in several places, and that the left eye was out of the socket. The foetus he found was around eight months old. There were deep wounds on the thigh of the body as well. It had been a truly vicious and brutal attack.

The judge passed sentence of death but Robinson insisted on his innocence. However, on the morning of his execution, he finally admitted his guilt and said that he had split Susannah's skull with an axe. On 20 July his neck was stretched and as Thomas Leman Rede noted, 'He died unpitied and unattended; for the brutality he had evinced had left him not one friend.'

41

RAPE OF A CHILD

Samuel Paramar, 8 August 1807

Over the centuries, sex crimes recorded at York offer us only a brief line explaining the offence. In 1379, for instance, one Edward Hewison was hanged there, and the note in the record, assembled in the late nineteenth century, simply says, 'A criminal guilty of rape.' Edward Hughes (see chapter 33), was convicted of rape and we know more about him than most. The offence occurs only rarely in these records, though there were two hangings of men convicted of rape in the early years of the nineteenth century.

Samuel Paramar was seventy years old when, at the Summer Assizes of 1807, he was convicted of raping a girl under ten years of age; he was also charged with attempted rape. We have to assume that the children in question soon made known what had happened, and clearly knew their attacker, because he was arrested and charged within a few days of the offences. He was tried before Baron Wood and the affair was soon dealt with; the death sentence was passed and the hanging date was fixed as 8 August 1807. He died alongside John Robinson (see chapter 40).

Eight years later, twenty-one-year-old Mark Bramah and George White were hanged for rape too, their victims also being children. They died on 5 August 1815.

42

HIGHWAY ROBBERY AT OULTON

James Winterbottom, 9 March 1808

James Winterbottom was one of the lowest forms of robbers on the roads and lanes of the county; his habit was to hang around inns, watch for men who had taken a few drinks too many and then waylay and rob them as they staggered homewards. He was reputedly a renegade and never settled to a job. He wanted easy money and a riotous life. Robbery was the quickest way to attain these things.

On 14 November near Oulton, Winterbottom's chosen victim was William Newton – and he was to be the last. Newton was a pedlar and was on his way home on that fateful night when he stopped at the Mason's Arms. There, he spoke with Winterbottom, as they knew each other. At about eight o'clock that evening, Newton left the inn. He said that after a few minutes he met the robber, who greeted him, passed by, and then struck him from behind. Newton said that he spoke to his attacker, saying, 'Jem, be quiet, I know thee!' But he said that Winterbottom carried on a vicious attack, knocking him to the ground. Newton said he was beaten till he was 'all in a gore'.

The robber stole the pedlar's licence, along with two guinea notes and a £1 note. But Newton was a formidable man; he shouted after Winterbottom that he had gold if he would come back for it. The judge at York asked him why he had done this, and the pedlar replied that 'I wished him to come back, for the bleeding had sobered me; and in another tussle I doubt not that I should have proved the better man.' Newton followed his attacker to the inn, and there the landlord and others put together the story. Men went back to look for a stolen pocket book (with the licence in it) and they eventually found it under a flagstone. Winterbottom was taken to justice and charged.

In York he was found guilty and was hanged on 9 March 1808..

43

THE YORKSHIRE WITCH

Mary Bateman, 20 March 1809

Mary Bateman is the arch-poisoner of Yorkshire murder, her reputation being endorsed by several Victorian writers who retold her story long after her death at York. She was from Aisenby, near Thirsk, and was destined to attain the dubious fame as the subject of ballads and chapbooks, even on the eve of her execution. Often called the 'Yorkshire Witch', she dabbled in fortune-telling and gradually began to see the advantages of bullying and bribing poor, gullible or weak victims. She also had a skill in putting on an image of having quasi-medical knowledge and indulging in some acts of abortion. But her downfall began when

Winterbottom's attack on Newton. (York Castle, 1831)

she promoted her 'health cure' in Leeds and administered something that caused the death of a Mrs Perigo.

Bateman's potions killed Mrs Perigo and there was a furore. Questions were asked and the law caught up with her. When Bateman was brought to trial, it was not difficult to find her guilty of wilful murder and she was sentenced to hang. Yet even in York Castle awaiting her fate she worked hard to find a means of escape; her most potentially successful ruse was to 'plead her belly'. For this to be proved, a panel of women were assembled to examine Bateman in order to ascertain the truth of her assertion – not a welcome prospect for most. Behind locked doors, the examination took place and she was found to be lying. There was no way out then.

Even in her cell, Bateman indulged in machinations to 'work magic' on other young women. But her evil came to an end at five o'clock on a chilly Monday morning in March 1809, when she was taken from her cell. The gaoler, who had been with her on her last night, noted that she wrote a letter to her husband and sent her wedding ring home to be given to

Mary Bateman, the Yorkshire Witch. (York Castle, 1831)

her daughter. She had her youngest child in her cell with her, to suckle, and it was a scene that the gaoler noted with feelings of sympathy. He also remarked on her silence regarding the crimes she had committed – and felt sure that she knew much more about other suspicious deaths connected with her activities.

At this time, noted killers attracted great crowds at their death, and Mary Bateman was no exception. Though there were no friends to swing on her legs to quicken her death, there was, nevertheless, a crowd to prove her status as a celebrity. A massive crowd had travelled from Leeds, where she had murdered Mrs Perigo, to see justice done. The hanging took place behind the 'new drop' and it was eerily quiet when Mary said a prayer, but a shudder went through the crowd when she begged for mercy and shouted that she was innocent.

As a coda to her story, we may note that Dr William Hey, of Leeds Infirmary, saw a chance to do some fund-raising, and he charged the public money to enter the hospital to see her body before dissection. He raised £80 and 14s.

44

THE DELINQUENTS HAD GROWN
TOO BOLD

Joseph Brown, 20 March 1809

Joseph Brown was always going to be a criminal: what we know of him makes it plain that he was always in the midst of trouble and on most occasions, he was the cause of it. He was Yorkshire born, but when he was young he went to London and there fell in with a rake named Hazelgrove, who all accounts agree was 'a remarkably fine young man but of idle habits.' The two men wheedled their way into hanging around a tavern linked to suttlery, or army supplies. There was a sideline in such places of prostitution, and so the men soon learned the ways of the world in most of the criminal aspects of what we now think of as the Regency 'underworld'.

They managed to avoid the law for a while, though they indulged in such schemes as extortion by threats and then fraud. They soon realised that London was too 'hot' for them and they came north. They took to the roads and inns across Yorkshire and were smart operators for some time, working anywhere from Huddersfield to Hull. But after one arrest and a gaol term, Brown was put into one of the prison hulks. There he is reckoned to have had terrible dreams, all saturated with the guilt of his wild life. But this had come too late: he had, by then, committed the crime that was to take him to the gallows.

Brown was charged with the murder of Elizabeth Fletcher and he pleaded not guilty. A witness stated that he was in a tavern with Brown and Hazelgrove when they were drinking with the victim and her sister. He said that Brown poured some unsweetened ale into a mug and gave it to Elizabeth to drink. The next morning, a Mrs Longbottom found the body, and also her sister, Sara, who was in a deep sleep. When Sara awoke, she had no idea what had happened to them both. Another witness said that Brown had told him he intended to marry Elizabeth because she was worth £20. Apparently, he and Hazelgrove, though they were both already married, had told everyone that they were single. Another sister, Rebecca, told how a box with valuables in it had been stolen from the sisters and that she had seen it in Brown's room.

A druggist said that the men had come to him for laudanum, but even more sensationally, he had in his possession a written confession from Brown in which he said that he had put a large quantity of laudanum into Sara Fletcher's beer at the public house in Ferrybridge where they were staying. He had also written: 'The former died early on the morning of the 22 October. We broke open her box and took out one guinea and a half. We were apprehended, heard before a magistrate, and discharged as he thought the evidence against us insufficient.'

There had also been an alleged confession of another murder, of a Selby carrier. It was all decided swiftly – Brown was guilty and must die. He was hanged along with Mary Bateman (see chapter 43), protesting his innocence.

45

TRIED UNDER A BLACK ACT

Jonathan Graham, 8 April 1809

Jonathan Graham, after shooting his father-in-law, reasoned that no one would suspect him because no one saw him shoot him. Such was the crazed and illogical reasoning that led him to the gallows. Graham was born in 1784 to a good family, and he married into a wealthy farming family named Jeft. To the objective eye, the future would have been bright for him, and so it was, but a wild urge to get rich well before any inheritance came his way led him to take his gun and to try and kill Mr Jeft.

Graham had become the general manager of Jeft's farm; his wife bore him a son, and so the future must have seemed assured: he was clearly the man who would take over from Mr Jeft eventually. But through sheer avarice, Graham wanted everything immediately rather than in some distant future. On 11 February 1809 he shot Mr Jeft, and within three weeks he was sanding trial for the murder.

He was tried under the Black Act, a law of 1723 which encompassed all kinds of capital crimes, including one of malicious wounding. The witnesses all came forward and the narrative of the attempted murder was put together. Graham went to borrow a gun from a man named Hartley, and on the second attempt, he had been able to use one of Harley's guns. The reason that the attempt failed was that Jeft had walked out of his house, where Graham had planned to shoot him, and thus the shot was made more difficult. As one witness said, 'If William Jeft had not come out the man would have shot him in the house through the window.' The whole affair was a serious piece of incompetence. Graham had made a mess of his plans for an alibi, and it was obvious to everyone what he had planned to do.

The Black Act that condemned him followed crimes committed in the eighteenth century in which men blackened their faces at night before carrying out robberies. The whole idea behind this was that the *motive* was judged and punished, not the outcome. On 8 April 1809, Graham was hanged, and apparently he showed no signs of remorse.

46

HANGED AT THE CITY GAOL

David Anderson, 12 August 1809

David Anderson was a Scot, and he had come to York just six months before he was arrested on a charge of uttering coin and notes of the realm. He had been a businessman back home but this had failed. He moved south to start again, and when he was mixed up with a character named Dent, he crossed the line into criminality. The trial and execution were at the City Gaol, and he was tried before Judge Chambre with a city jury present.

Port Arthur penitentiary, Tasmania, where many forgers were destined. (Author's collection)

When Anderson was first suspected, his lodgings were searched and almost £130 in £1 notes were found. The scenario is the oldest in crime history: Dent turned King's evidence and brought about Anderson's ruin. He had two 'fatal notes' in his possession when he was caught – notes made from copperplates by Dent.

Not since April 1794 had anyone suffered death after a trial at the City Gaol, and the last occasion had been barbaric in the extreme: a man named Waddingham had been dragged on a hurdle across Ousebridge and taken to be hanged at the Tyburn. Now, here was Anderson on the scaffold and he was openly praying and asking for some hope of forgiveness in the 'better world' to come. He spoke of Dent and referred to him as the 'man who had first led him into this fatal connexion.' He said that Dent had employed him to produce the plates, and that this man would have his blood on his hands.

Uttering was a very serious offence at the time, though executions were rare. Between 1800 and 1834, there were only two persons hanged for the crime, from over sixty charges and trials. The majority of culprits were sent to Van Dieman's Land for long periods of penal servitude.

47

A CLOTHIER COMMITS FRAUD

John Senior, 21 March 1810

In the 1820s, people thought about the massive South Sea Bubble of 1720, a nationwide speculation in shares which ended in ruin and misery for so many. It brought to mind the stigma of the fraudulent bankrupt, though there are very few cases of bankruptcy ending in executions in the chronicles of hanging. One of the few was a man named John Senior, who pleaded not guilty to concealing property above the value of £20, with intent to defraud his creditors. He had become bankrupt in early 1810 with debts of £1,184.

Senior was a Yorkshire clothier by trade, and for some time he was successful and respected, working much of the time with the racing fraternity around York and Doncaster. However, he started gambling, in addition to what we would now call networking, and he had significant losses. Desperate, he began to commit fraud; this was during the war with Napoleon, and for people who had to handle paper money, it was not difficult to obtain loans. His debts mounted, and he had obtained goods of around £2,000 in value. But he then concealed some of these during his bankruptcy, and that fact was discovered.

A man named Illingworth recalled being given large quantities of a cloth called kerseymere by Senior and asked to store them; he then brought more, including a web of cloth. These items were taken off the premises at night for secret storage. Senior had given a public oath when he was first examined, stating that he had no possessions other than those declared. The law could do nothing to those who had abetted him: Senior was solely responsible and he paid with his life. The bill that condemned him was made law in the reign of George II; many thought that its application was outmoded and that it should have been repealed.

48

SEVENTEEN LUDDITES DIE

George Mellor & others, 8 & 16 January 1813

In 1812, the clothing industry of the West Riding faced the implications of the arrival of new machinery in the finishing processes of clothing manufacture, and many of them did so with a resolve to fight the mechanisation. What some of them did in their zeal to survive was to bring a reign of terror to villages and mills from the Pennines to the Halifax and Bradford areas. In order to defeat them, the forces of law had to bring in the militia, such was the fear across the county. The year 1812 was a time of particularly strained and repressive economic measures and poorer families were suffering. It might seem strange to mention that many of the Luddites were quite well off, but they feared the future and they did not stand idly by while the greater macroeconomic factors crushed them.

The Luddites took their name from a fabled character named Ned Ludd, who reputedly led similar machine-wrecking attacks in Nottingham. A leader appeared on the scene in the Spen Valley, who was to conduct a campaign of profound fear-instilling aggression against those employers who had new machinery installed. The focus for the campaign was the trade linked to the cloth finishing processes, in particular the shearers, of whom Mellor was one. This was a skilled business, demanding the expert use of large and unwieldy shears for trimming and finishing.

Mellor realised that the essence of success in these attacks was secrecy, because the communities along the valleys where the clothing industry flourished would all know each other well from communal occasions. He therefore had his men black their faces and always wear hats, and they would then attack by night. The reign of terror lasted for some time and the local magistrates were at a loss what to do, but the chain of command broadened and the reaction of the authorities spread from the West Riding to the militia, and then to the Lord Lieutenant of the county at Wentworth Woodhouse, and eventually to the Home Secretary.

After various delays, which gave the Luddites the upper hand, sheer paranoia eventually led to positive action; first it was due to military successes, as a brutal and repressive group of militia conducted their own reprisals, and then, with the new Home Secretary, Lord Sidmouth, taking his place at the Home Office, the establishment began to create an equal measure of fear in the Luddites. Soon it was a case of the magistrates finding men willing to give information, and Sidmouth was keen on the use of spies functioning as *agents provocateurs*.

Matters were made worse as deaths occurred: notably, there had been the murder of a factory-owner named Horsfall, and Mellor, along with William Thorpe and Thomas Smith, were charged. Horsfall had been attacked on the road, shot by men positioned alongside in undergrowth. Witnesses came forward to implicate Mellor, a man who had also been pointed at by a particular turncoat and petty thief from the village of Flockton. The three men were convicted of murder and found guilty. One commentator writing in the 1830s wrote: 'It is impossible to read the details of this and the other Luddite cases without shuddering at the cold-hearted and systematic manner in which the murders were debated and agreed on . . . '

Mellor, Smith and Thorpe were hanged on 8 January 1813. They were led to the scaffold still in their irons; they all went down on their knees after the chaplain asked them to pray. Mellor said, 'Some of my enemies may be here. If they be, I freely forgive them, and all the world, and I hope the world will forgive me.' The bodies were taken to York County Hospital for dissection.

On 16 January, fourteen men were hanged on the conviction of taking illegal oaths and the destruction of a mill, with an additional charge of riot. Eight men were found guilty of riot and destruction at Cartwright's Mill, the story featuring in Charlotte Bronte's novel, *Shirley*. There were attempts to provide alibis and several defence witnesses were called, but all that failed, and it took the jury just five minutes to decide on a guilty verdict. As noted by several historians in earlier times, all the men were married and all left young children fatherless. The word 'Luddite' entered the language, such was the impact of that year of terror when the middle classes in the valleys of the West Riding could not sleep easily in their beds.

49

MURDER OF A SHERIFF'S OFFICER

John James, 31 March 1814

John James had a small farm at West Witton, and in 1813 he was a man under severe pressure. One reason for this was the sheriff's officer in the area, a man named Ridley. The officer, according to the trial evidence, pressurised the farmer in a variety of ways; things came to a head when Ridley put in a distress for rent which was not at that time due. The part played by the landlord is not entirely clear, so we will never know whether the landlord and the sheriff together harassed the farmer, but whatever the case , the motives of the officer appear to be very low indeed.

Ridley wanted to satisfy a nasty and deep feeling of spite, and more mundanely, he wanted to sell off James's stock at short notice. This all amounted to oppression, and the worm turned. From James's point of view, he had been robbed – of cattle and of corn. What he faced was

Right: *The Dumb Steeple, a meeting point for the Luddites.* (Author's collection)

Below: *Mellor attacks Horsfall.* (L. Rede)

one difficult form of legal redress known as replevin, an action that meant he would have had to apply to the County Court and pay all costs incurred, with no guarantee of success, simply to have his goods returned to him. He would have to prove the illegal actions of a legal official – a seemingly impossible task. What was left for him, in order to hit back, but crime? He shot and killed Ridley on 24 November 1813, and then gave himself up to the authorities.

James did not plead guilty to murder, however. People testified that Ridley had been attacked by James on some occasions; one man heard James say that Ridley had taken away his corn and that he would be revenged. In defence, James saw his actions as defending his property and his life. What was confirmed, however, was that no rent was due, and Ridley had indeed acted illegally; Ridley had sold £4 worth of hay for just 15s – to himself. So he had officially purchased distrained goods which he had obtained.

But murder was proved. Clearly James had the intention to take Rdley's life. On 31 March 1814, in his last moments, John James said, 'I am going out of this sinful world for protecting my property, and many a bright pound have I lost beside that . . . Christ have mercy upon me!'

50

TRANQUIL ON THE SCAFFOLD

Robert Turner, 31 March 1814

John James did not die alone that day in March. Robert Turner died with him, having been convicted of murdering Margaret Appleby by administering poison to her. He pleaded not guilty, but there was little hope that he could save his neck that day. It was a story which was very common through the centuries: an illegitimate child affiliated on the man alleged to be involved. Margaret was about to obtain an order from the local magistrates to have Turner taken in for charging and for the following binds secured. But on the way to the magistrate, Turner met her and they spoke. He then tried to persuade her to leave the matter, and they went for a drink. It was a situation we find on innumerable occasions in the records of petty sessions across the land.

In the public house, he bought Margaret a drink. She was seized with a vomiting fit soon after drinking it and died. This was followed by the usual course of events: suspicion was cast on Turner, and then a surgeon carried out an autopsy, though the telltale evidence of poison which should have been present – was not. The problem was that Turner had absconded and had gone north to South Shields, where he was eventually found, hiding in a cupboard. He was brought back to York, and in spite of the absence of any poison found in Margaret's body, his flight from justice indicated his guilt as far as the jury were concerned, and he was found guilty of wilful murder. The two facts seemed a paradox: there was no evidence against him but a flight from justice was proven: it was too much to overlook or try to understand in any way except by perceiving guilt.

It was noted that Turner's behaviour in prison was 'indecorous', this meant that he resisted all treatment and fought against restraint. He also protested his innocence to the last moment, but then, on the scaffold, he was 'tranquil' and put his head in the noose, a job usually left to the hangman.

THE GENTLEMAN ATTORNEY HANGS

Joseph Blackburn, 8 April 1815

The narrative of Joseph Blackburn's trip to the scaffold is highly unusual within this melancholy list of malefactors. The reason for this is that, in 1793, when he married a woman of 'respectable connections' while in his twenties, all seemed to offer him a bright future as a Leeds attorney. For twenty years he prospered in his profession and was well respected. But then a man who had been in his employment as a clerk put forward some serious allegations: that Blackburn had taken stamps from old deeds and placed them on new ones, and that he had also changed the value of the stamps in this context.

There was evidence and Blackburn was brought to trial. The charge was that he had 'feloniously forged and counterfeited the resemblance of certain stamps used by the Commissioner of Stamps.' Under a statute of George III (1808), referring to mortgage deeds, this was a capital offence. Blackburn pleaded not guilty. It was destined to be a long and complex trial, heard by Sir Simon le Blanc, and the money gained by Blackburn in the case was around £180 – a very large sum then, perhaps equal to £12,000 at today's value.

Several witnesses were called, including Abraham Smith, a stamper from the London Stamp Office, who said that no stamps were ever issued separate from the parchment in a deed, nor could stamps be issued on their own. Smith inspected the deeds in question and stated that they were counterfeit. This was corroborated by William Kappen, also of the Stamp Office. Then Robert Barr, a writer in the Town Clerks' Office, went to inspect Blackburn's office and property; there he found a quantity of small stamps. Even worse for Blackburn, a Leeds engraver deposed that he had done work for Blackburn, not knowing exactly what purpose was intended, simply writing, 'This Indenture' on the plates given.

It was looking black indeed for the Leeds attorney. There were attempts by the defence to mount legal objections, but in the end the prisoner himself was allowed to speak after Le Blanc had overruled all objections. He said, after a lengthy explanation, that, 'the deed in question had upon it a regular stamp when it was executed in my office . . . Gentlemen, my life is in your hands.' Over twenty witnesses spoke about Blackburn's character, but the jury retired and after only fifteen minutes they returned with a guilty verdict.

When sentence was passed, the judge made a point of stressing that Blackburn was in 'an honourable profession' and that the 'thirst for money' had corrupted him. When sentence of death was passed, Blackburn was convulsed in agony and had to be carried out of the court. It was a case of some marked notoriety, particularly after a petition asking for clemency was signed by 3,000 'respectable persons', as the writer Leman Rede wrote. But Lord Sidmouth, the Home Secretary, would not yield to pressure.

Blackburn, in his last moments, joined in a prayer and said, before the drop fell: 'Oh Lord Almighty, have mercy upon me and preserve my soul alive!' But it was a botched hanging and the poor man struggled in pain for two minutes while the executioner adjusted the tangled rope; in all, it took almost seven minutes for Blackburn to die. He was buried at Rothwell, near Leeds.

52

A KILLING IN ARUNDEL PLACE

William King, 31 July 1817

William King was a tool-maker of Sheffield, and he was seen by a neighbour on the evening of 4 June 1817 in a distressed state. He appeared to be ill. But then there was a terrific row heard from his house some time later and he was found holding a bloody poker, standing near the bed where his victim, Sarah Trippett, lay dead. Beside her was a small child. When asked by a neighbour what he had done, King reacted violently and would have killed the man, as he was still in a murderous rage.

Word of the atrocity soon spread and the community was out in the street, baying for King to come down; eventually he did so, still holding the poker. When the local constable came on the scene, King explained his actions, saying that he was jealous, and that he had been drinking, having had a long session in his cups at the Swan with two Necks down the road. His poor victim was still clinging on to life as King was led in handcuffs to the cell. Sarah did die, and King was shortly sent to York to stand trial for murder. He stood before Baron Wood and his story soon emerged. He had known Sarah for five years, and although she was married, she and King had started a home together. But her husband returned to Sheffield.

Witnesses painted a picture of King as an aggressive drunk; one man said he was 'sullen and fondish of ale.' But there was no question of insanity. He had intended to take Sarah's life and had done so most brutally. King was sentenced to hang, and it was reported that in the death cell he was 'in a melancholy stupor.' He left his very violent world on 31 July 1817.

53

ROBBERY OF THE SQUIRE

Joseph Pickersgill, 12 August 1818

Jospeh Pickersgill was born in 1787 and followed his father into the hard labour of being a banksman. We know little about him, other than that he married in 1810, and that he then stepped over the line into the world of criminality, his robbing finally leading to an attack on a Mr Squire Ramsden on the road near Wakefield, taking a pocket-book and some silver. But Pickersgill was a violent man as well, and his attack was vicious.

Ramsden went to Wakefield market on 5 May 1818, and had been enjoying a drink in a public house when Pickersgill came in. They knew each other and Ramsden asked Pickersgill to walk home with him, but the latter said he had other business to attend to. A woman named Mary Norton, who worked at Pickersgill's pit, walked some of the way home with Ramsden, but then left him. Shortly after, he sensed someone behind him and before he knew it he was being punched. He said at the trial, 'I was knocked down, and the person who knocked me down began to punch me on the head and face with his feet. I cried out for help . . . I knew the voice. It was that of Joseph Pickersgill.' The attacker had told him to 'Giver over' and had then put his knee to the back of his victim's neck and took the man's pocket-book.

Poor Ramsden, in agony, said, 'Thou hast gotten my money, let me die quietly.' But Pickersgill insisted that there was more money hidden on Ramsden and he wrenched him around to take a purse. It was a cut-and-dried case in York, and a guilty verdict was soon reached. After being told he was to die, Pickersgill begged for mercy as he had a wife and children. But the judge said, 'You see the dreadful state into which you have plunged your family . . . I entreat you to prepare for that awful fate which . . . awaits you.' It was an occasion on which the judge took the opportunity to expatiate at length on the awful consequences of rash and desperate criminal acts, notably in such hard times. Apparently, the man showed firmness 'but no bravado' on the scaffold.

54

FATHER & SON HANG FOR HIGHWAY ROBBERY

Thomas & William Hickman, 2 April 1819

When a writer in 1829 reflected on the lives of these two villains, he quoted an old saying: 'Accustom yourself to privation, and habit will make it necessary.' He was prompted to be moralistic because the Hickmans' crime and their subsequent ruin were put down to drink. To pay for his liquor, Thomas Hickman took to the road with weapons and determination to collect the money he urgently needed.

The Hickmans lived in the village of Newton, close to Wakefield, though as to the nature of the father and son and their crimes, there are conflicting stories. Thomas, the father, and William, the son, were by some accounts men with a long history of petty crime on the highroads around Wakefield. All kinds of thefts were accredited to them. But a local constable, after the crime for which the two men hanged, claimed that this specific attack was their first – and done in a mood of utter desperation. The former account seems more likely, as the attack was not the work of amateurs or beginners.

The two men bought pistols and made masks on the day before the highway robbery, which was their capital offence. They robbed Thomas Serle and William Lord after Serle had enjoyed a day at Pontefract market; he took home with him a large amount of silver and six guinea notes. He was riding in a covered cart, leaving Pontefract at dusk, and when Lord came up with him, they agreed to travel on together. A short time later, the Hickmans rushed at them from a hedge, bearing pistols and shouting 'Deliver thy money!' Serle said in court, 'I gave them some silver . . . but they were not content.' Lord drove off as soon as the robbers appeared, intending to hide his money. But after he offered them just 18d, they found his silver hidden under potatoes in his cart. The Hickmans took everything they could carry and retreated, guns still brandished.

The pursuit of the highway robbers was not difficult; the next day, the local constable, on being told of these events, immediately thought of the Hickmans. Constable Shaw told the court that he went to search for Hickman, and found the provincial notes stolen from Serle. He added, 'I also found on William Hickman the key of a pistol, and the key of Thomas Hickman's stable door. In the room there was a basket in which I found a quantity of silver.'

The Hickmans made it into the Old Bailey Sessions Papers, achieving notoriety. (Newgate Calendar)

In Thomas Hickman's house the constable found two pistols and a powder flask. The elder Hickman confessed to everything.

Serle identified the prisoners by their voices; and apparently their gait was also 'very peculiar' and so, along with the other evidence and the suspicions of Shaw, the father and son were tried and found guilty. The two men were hanged on 2 April 1819.

55

TANKERSLEY GAMEKEEPER KILLED

Samuel Booth, 30 March 1820

Samuel Booth, along with accomplices William Garrett and Benjamin Bower, went poaching. It was their usual habit, and the result of a night out in the wild was normally a few rabbits. But on the night of 10 October 1819, the poaching led to murder.

The men were stopped by two keepers, Joseph Parkin and his brother, Thomas, who were out to find poachers that night; at four o'clock in the morning they saw four men walking towards them and Thomas called out to Garrett, 'What my lad, is it you?' He put his hand on Garrett's shoulder. After that, things turned nasty. Booth was accused of having a pocket full of small knives. Booth turned around and shot Thomas Parkin dead.

Then Joseph Parkin was attacked by all the poachers, and he recalled that Booth had struck him on the head and shoulder with the butt of a gun. He heard a voice say, 'Hit him or stick him!' and heard a gun go off. When he came around, he tried to get help for Thomas, but it was too late. The surgeon, Mr Stonefield, testified that the shot that killed Thomas had put a bullet through his left side and had exited through his back. Booth tried to tell the constable who came for him that the gun had fired by accident.

In court, it was a matter of ascertaining what the others had actually done on that fateful night. The jury were satisfied that Booth was the man who had shot Thomas Parkin, and the judge pressed for opinions on the matter of whether or not the others had 'been engaged in the same transaction, and went out determined to join in . . .' Nothing was resolved on that issue, and while Booth was found guilty and sentenced to hang, the others were respited and transported for life.

56

A HUSBAND POISONED

Ann Barber, 19 March 1821

James Barber died of arsenic poisoning in 1821, and his wife was the only suspect. An Oulton doctor, John Hindle, was thorough in his trade, and at the inquest (held at Barber's house), Hindle went to work. He found extensive evidence of poison in the corpse. He stated later in court that he had taken white arsenic from the coating of the stomach. He said, 'I know of no other substance that would make the lungs so very black . . . I have seen persons poisoned, and their external appearance agreed with Barber's.'

The defence tried to make the most of Hindle's lack of experience in these matters, but the fact was that Ann Barber had been having an affair with a man who lodged in the family home, and the jury saw that as the central and determining fact in the case. Ann Barber had a motive. In the community, there was evidence that there had been some disturbance in the neighbourhood about a man named Thompson (who was the lodger).

When Jane Smirthwaite, a friend of Barber's, gave evidence, she said that she had called a neighbour, Sarah Parker, on the evening before the death, as James Barber had been saying he was going to die. But other details began to emerge at that point, such as the fact that Barber had fallen from a cart in the street. It seems highly likely that there had been worries about noise and violence in the streets around the Barber home, the cause of which had been the traditional 'rough music' in which communities expressed their moral disapproval of such things as affairs and adultery. Paradoxically, it seems that Barber himself had had just as much taunting as Thompson and Ann.

But all this was a diversion from the fact that Ann had bought mercury, as a constable testified. She confessed that she had given her husband a quantity of this in some warm ale, saying that she was 'stalled of him'. There was only a flimsy defence, and the judge clarified the issues involved when he said that there was evidence that Ann Barber had intended to kill her husband. The jury stated that she was guilty of petit treason and murder. The judge then said to Ann, 'As far as my understanding can judge, no reasonable creature can have any doubt about your guilt.'

A week later, on the scaffold, one witness noted that 'there was nothing interesting in her countenance.' The only fortunate element in the case is that Ann was spared the horrendous death of being dragged in a cart and burned. It was noted that 'she received spiritual consolation and died without a struggle.'

Ann Barber, from an old print. (Author's collection)

57

BRUTAL KILLING OUTSIDE A PUB

James Mosley, 6 April 1822

This is the sad tale of a death over a Banbury cake. In a tavern called the Harrow in Sheffield, in 1821, two men fell out over a cake. A group of grinders had gone into the pub for a drink and one of them, a man named Beuley, ordered a cake. When James Mosley, who had been in another room, also came for a cake, there was an altercation and Mosley had to be held back from assaulting Beuley. It was not the end of the matter for Mosley, who went away to find himself a knife. He was heard to say: 'Damn him, I'll stick him!' as he walked off from the butcher's shop with a knife.

Mosley waited outside the Harrow for the grinders to come out, hiding the knife under his coat. When they did, he was watching for Beuley, and when he lunged, the knife missed the intended victim and cut into a man named Mackay, who was rushed to hospital. It took him a long time to die.

Charged with murder, Mosley was arrested and stood trial at York in March 1822. The developments in this were most unusual, but they provide a scenario often seen in trials for murder: the dead man had a fatal disease, so did the stabbing actually cause his death? This was worth consideration, of course, because the man had experienced a slow death in hospital. The surgeon who gave testimony stated that there was no evidence that the stabbing had directly caused death. But this was in the 1820s, before the number of capital offences were reduced, and although Mosley was acquitted of murder, he could be re-tried with a charge of cutting and maiming with intent to take life.

After another five-hour trial on the new charge, the jury found the case clear-cut and soon returned a guilty verdict. There was no doubt that Mosley had intended to kill or at least seriously injure his intended victim, and the judge said, with that in mind, he had waited to 'wreak his vengeance'. Mosley was hanged on 6 April 1822, leaving a wife and two children to struggle in life without him.

58

A QUARRY ROBBERY

Isaac Charlesworth, 13 August 1825

On 5 July 1825, John Green heard a shout of 'Murder!' at a quarry at Dyer's Bridge, Sheffield. As two men ran past him he managed to knock down the second, but the other hit him with a pistol. Another man then arrived on the scene and saw Green staggering and bleeding.

The two men who had been running had dropped two hats and a pistol. This gun was to provide the death warrant for Isaac Charlesworth.

The pistol was recognised and Charlesworth was arrested the next day. Green identified him as the man who was running and who had turned to hit him. A story was put together, which began with the arrival of Halifax man Joseph Cropper in Sheffield on the night of the attack at a public house, the Coach and Horses in Water Lane. Cropper had wanted a drink and also asked where a certain woman could be found. A group of men drinking in the pub, including Charlesworth, persuaded the landlady to serve him and acted friendly toward him. When they offered to take him to the place where the woman lived, he trusted them, which was nearly a fatal mistake.

Charlesworth and another man took Cropper to the quarry, where they beat and robbed him. But thanks to Green and the coach driver who came to help, Charlesworth was soon in the hands of the law. It had been a violent and bloody night's events, one attack after another.

In York, the case was heard by Baron Hullock, and was uncomplicated: Charlesworth was found guilty of highway robbery and of attempted murder. The judge had no hesitation in passing the death sentence. Charlesworth, who never gave the name of the other man who was with him that night, and who had attacked Cropper, said as he was taken away: 'Please ye, my Lord, the last words I shall say on the scaffold will be that I have been murdered by means of perjured men.'

59

FATHER & SON MURDER TEAM

William & John Dyon, 21 February 1828

William Dyon and his son John harboured a hatred of William's brother, also called John, and accounts confirm that of these two murderers, William engendered in his son an irrational hatred of his uncle. The enmity grew over the years until one day, when it appeared that young John had been robbed of his inheritance, William determined to take the life of his brother.

The killers planned the attack carefully, and had an assistant named White who helped them store some arms ready for an attack on the unsuspecting John Dyon. They had left the guns in position eight days before Dyon came home on 16 February, and set about him after his day at Doncaster market. John Dyon had left Doncaster with two friends, but they left him at the top of Austerfield Lane and Dyon rode to his home at Brancroft alone. One writer at the time calculated that he was only 800yds from home when the killers struck. He was shot by his gate as he dismounted his horse to open it. His own brother and nephew had taken his life.

A servant found Dyon's mare at the gate and then, later, he and another man found the corpse. An inquest was held, and there was some suspicion cast towards the Dyons, as the enmity between the brothers was well known in the area. But a verdict of 'wilful murder by person or persons unknown' was returned. However, the Dyons were interviewed and they provided an alibi. But there was a reward offered for information leading to the arrest of the killers, and a man named White came forward, spoke to the magistrate, Denison, and the Dyons were arrested.

We have to feel for the father of the two brothers; his favourite had been killed, and his other son arrested for the murder. But within a few days, the Dyons were in the dock in York. The surgeon gave an account of how John had died: a bullet had penetrated his left side, by a rib, and had passed through the lungs. He had removed a bullet from the left shoulder blade, and when examined, the man had been dead for perhaps six hours. White was the one with most to say, naturally. He had been a labourer to the dead man, and it seems possible that he fabricated much of the story he told at York, as it reads in such an embellished way. White said that they told him they had come to murder his master, that he had got their property and they could bear it no longer.

Other witnesses then explained how a feeble alibi had been arranged; some overheard words being said that set up an alibi within friends and family. It was even reported that William Dyon had said to one man, 'We are going to shoot your master tonight and if you tell I'll shoot you all.' The magistrate and another man both spoke of tracing the steps of two men from the Dyon gate to a distance of 16ft, and that they knew that William Dyon 'walked with his toes turned out' and the marks left suggested that manner of footprint.

There was no real defence, and when William Dyon was asked what he had to say, he replied that he left that to his counsel. The defence statements were very thin; merely remarks about there not being any guns around the house and that William Dyon was always in bed early. The jury took eight minutes to decide on a guilty verdict.

We have a close description of how these two died. William expressed a horror of being 'anatomised', which would have takn place. Before they died, John Dyon joined in a fervent prayer, but his father 'was entirely reckless' and looked across the faces in the crowd, as if searching for some he knew. John confessed his guilt when asked if he understood the justice of his sentence. But William glared at him and muttered something between his teeth. The son struggled for six minutes; William stooped to lengthen the rope. He knew how to hasten his end.

60

INFANTICIDE IN SHEFFIELD

Martin Slack, 30 March 1829

This is one of those Georgian cases that turns the stomach when it comes to the modern sensibility, because it deals with the execution of a teenager and with a difficult and intractable aspect of homicide in the social context of the time.

Martin Slack was just fifteen when his relationship with Elizabeth Haigh began. They were both from poor families, and so when the girl became pregnant, the parish officers made her take out an affiliation action against Martin. But his family did not want the couple to be together and he had no bail; his next stop was the Wakefield House of Correction. But when released, he still had no support from his family and was ordered to find the money to pay for the child's maintenance. He used to visit the mother and child, but was burning with resentment at paying the money. One morning when Martin was visiting, Elizabeth left the child with him on a sofa while she went upstairs. When she came down again, she picked up the child and saw smoke at its mouth. A strong, burning liquid then affected her own mouth and cheek as she came close to the baby.

Elizabeth screamed in shock, and cried for help. She yelled, 'You've poisoned her!' and when her mother arrived from down the street, she saw the horrible situation and a surgeon was called. He called for more help but by the evening, the child was dead. It was an easy task to find and apprehend Martin Slack, and the constable saw that there were burn marks on his fingers and clothes too. The post-mortem confirmed that death was by corrosive poison.

Acid burns were proved on Slack's clothes. The inquest found him guilty and he was committed for trial at York.

In 1829 at the Spring Assizes, Slack appeared before Baron Pollock. It was a clear-cut case and he was found guilty of murder. His only words were, 'Evidences which have come against me have been sworn falsely . . .' Pollock told him he could hold out no hope of mercy for the young man. In court, and later on, Slack raged and made little sense. He referred to the general feeling at home that he would be hanged and dissected. Then later, nearer his appointed time to die, he calmed down. He maintained his innocence to the last, and indeed, his body was cut down and taken to the surgeons for dissection.

61

HE KILLED HIS WOMAN

William Shaw, 12 March 1830

In March 1830, the body of Rachel Crossley was found in a coal pit at Kirkburton, Huddersfield. Everything indicated this was a case of murder, and the finger of suspicion pointed at her male friend and possible fiancé, William Shaw. The coroner, Thomas Lee, listened to a number of statements and to medical evidence. After that, Shaw was named as the perpetrator of a wilful murder. He was promptly committed to York Castle.

Shaw had been indicted for the murder of Rachel, the daughter of a poor coal miner. When her body was found, some of her bones were broken and her clothes were fastened and pinned in a strange way; the bruises and cuts were such that death would had to have been the result of an attack rather than a fall into the pit where she was found. One of William's friends had said, when the story emerged, 'Oh Bill, thou knows summat about it!' In court, Shaw said that he knew as much as anyone, but that did not help his case. What he had said, when first he spoke about what he had done, was, 'I wish someone would push my brains out.'

Rachel Crossley, the mother of the dead woman, said that she had applied for a warrant from the local overseers and that Shaw had first spoken about the business when he overheard some women talking in a public house about the death. After that, he was arrested, and in court he had nothing to say. The judge at York talked about the extreme brutality of the crime, and referred to the man's 'hardened cruelty'. Shaw was hanged within three days and his body was given to the surgeons.

62

A MURDEROUS DUO

Charles Turner & James Twibell, 30 April 1831

Jonathan Habbershon was a man with a responsible job at the *Deep Pit Colliery*, Sheffield. He was walking home late on 5 October 1830 when he was set upon by a gang of men armed

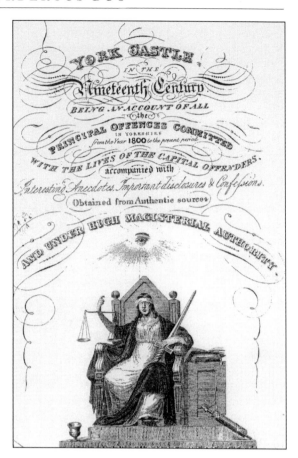

Frontispiece to Rede's York Castle,
1831, the first collection of York trials.
(Author's collection)

with hedge stakes and a flat iron. They thought he would have some money on him, and they were right. It wasn't much, but after they viciously attacked him, they took his watch and other small prizes and ran off. The man was almost dead, so severely beaten that there was no certainty that he would survive. But remarkably, he got to his feet and staggered towards home.

People met Habbershon and helped him home, where his wife tended him. The villains, Twibell, Turner and Priestley, met people they knew as they went through the dark parkland in the area. Naturally, they gave alibis, as meetings with them would be reported later. A surgeon named Ray came to help the injured man, and he later recalled walking past the scene of the attack and seeing a pool of blood and the hedge stake. But there had also been cuts to the victim's face. It had been a determined and brutal assault.

The robbers now had the task of selling the watch, and they went looking for a man named Butcher, and found him in a tavern called the Green Man. One of the robbers had sold his share in the watch by that time, and they were all haggling with Butcher when a constable entered the pub and started asking questions. When searched, the officer found crowns, pennies and a watch on Twibell, who claimed he had obtained them at Rotherham races. But they were arrested and, of course, the watch was identified.

In front of the magistrate, the ploy of hearing the men's stories regarding that night separately led to the sure belief that Twibell and Turner were the main culprits. They also had a deposition from the still severely ill Habbershon, whom, later, was well enough to see the suspects, but could not be sure about their identity. The turning point came when Turner confessed, being informed that 'turning King's evidence' would save him. He was wrong: pieces of evidence were put together and the magistrate committed both men to York.

Before Mr Justice Park, Priestley this time tried to take the chance of saving his life by telling the story of the others; confessions followed and of course, other accessories, including Butcher, saved their skins by giving clear testimony against the two main villains. Turner and Twibell were convicted of malicious assault and robbery. Park gave the speech about the 'full weight of the law' falling on them and put on the black cap. The hanging took place after a letter to Habbershon from the attackers had made the point that they would not have done it had they not been drunk. On the scaffold, they both prayed as the hoods were placed and they were speedily hanged. Their bodies were allowed to be taken home for burial.

63

MOTHER OF NINE EXECUTED, WITH TWO MEN

Mary Hunter, Ebenezer Wright & Thomas Law, 30 March 1833

This gallows tale began with a dispute over some horses in a pinfold at Lotherton, and involved a bitter hatred that Mary Hunter had for Mr Marshall, who had land in addition to the pinfold (a pound where stray animals were kept). Mary rowed with Marshall over a supposed 4d he owed her. The case went before a magistrate and she lost. Mary was heard to say, 'I'll be revenged if I hang for it.' There had been a fight over the affair before it was heard in court.

Mary tried all available methods to induce a servant girl named Hannah Gray to set fire to Marshall's haystacks. She threatened her and then offered money. In court, it was said that Mary promised Hannah a new frock if she would do it, and then later said she would 'tear her liver out' if she did not. At that time, there was rural crime across much of England: it was the time of the 'Captain Swing' riots and rural destruction, mainly across the eastern counties. Animals were maimed and haystacks set on fire, the trouble rooted in the deprivation suffered by farm labourers and the exploitation of poor labour by the rich land-holders. Mary Hunter had allowed something of that spirit to influence her when she thought of revenge.

One question was whether or not her husband, Thomas, was involved in the fire, but he was questioned and released. Then, a few days after the fire, three more stacks were burned. The epidemic of stack-burning also infected Ebenezer Wright, a young man who used that crime as revenge, as Mary had; he was angry at a solicitor named Oxley at Rotherham, who had led a prosecution against him. His accomplice, Norburn, had turned King's evidence and expected to be released, but at first both men were tried and sentenced to hang; then Norburn was reprieved.

Finally, there was another man on the scaffold with Mary Hunter. This was Thomas Law, who had committed highway robbery when he attacked a man named Atkinson on the road near Ferrybridge as he was returning from Pontefract market. Law inflicted twenty head wounds on the poor man and left him for dead. But amazingly, the victim recovered and he testified against Law, who was called a 'reckless and desperate man' by the reporter for *The Times*. Law's most memorable words before he died were, 'May the Devil get the witnesses, they have sworn most falsely against us!'

Mary Hunter, a mother of nine children, died at York alongside Ebenezer Wright and Thomas Law; it must have been a noisy and unrepentant trio on view that day as the crowds looked on.

64

THREE DIE TOGETHER

Thomas Rogers, Cook & Morrow, 26 April 1834

Thomas Rogers was an obscure character, a man whose name ignominiously goes into the York chronicle of death with the most maligned sex crime of buggery by his name; he committed that crime with a man he worked with, George Bennett. There are clearly some deep and considerable reasons why he confessed to that act, telling his employer about it. From that point it was a track to the gallows in the 1830s.

The great lawyer, Baron Alderson, sat in judgement at York, and he had words to say regarding this offence; he said it was one which caused human nature to 'shudder' and that 'it was one which struck at the root of the propagation of society and was one prohibited both by the laws of God and of man . . .' The judge was emotionally disturbed by having to pass sentence of death, and as for Rogers, he was silent all the time, even when he was led away.

There was an atmosphere of a feast day at the hanging. With Rogers were two others felons, Morrow and Cook. Under the beam, Morrow was in the middle. Rogers had the white cap placed on his head; then the second cap. Morrow was the last onto the scaffold and had to stand while adjustments were made to the others: but eventually all were dropped and it is on record that they took a while to die: Morrow, it was noted, died in great agony.

65

SUICIDE THWARTED IN THE

DEATH CELL

William Allott, Ursula Lofthouse & Joseph Heeley, 6 April 1835

William Allott was a thoroughly unlikable character who ran a dairy farm; he lived with Martha Hardwick and a milk boy, Joseph Wolstenholme, and liked to use his fists. Martha was the usual recipient of his temper and his blows. Allott also enjoyed his drink, and when he took out legal action against his own sister in September 1834, he spent the day at a public house, no doubt to enjoy the moment, such was his twisted hatred.

One day in April 1835, young Joseph carried out his chores alone at the farm; later he saw Martha and then went out to play. Allott's drinking that day led to his character totally changing: he became a rampant monster, and several people saw and heard him raging that day, particularly when he started shouting that Martha was robbing him every day and that she was a whore. A file forger named Rainey heard all this; then later, when Joseph returned home from play, he saw Allott, his clothes soaked in blood, carrying Martha to the bed. Allott said that she was drunk, but as the boy had been out, Allott asked, 'What hast thou been doing to get our mistress knocked on the head?' Allott was trying to put together an alibi for himself, whilst shifting the blame onto Joseph.

But Joseph observed everything and saw that the man's shoes had hair on them as well as blood. That was important later, of course. Nobody had called for help and a long period of time had passed since young Joseph came home. But now a constable called Boler was named and Allott spun him a tale of two supposed men seen running over the fields, coming from the farmhouse. The poor woman was still slowly dying and asking for help; a surgeon was called for, but she died soon after. The constable had a close inspection of the scene of crime; he saw that there had been a struggle, with a broken chair and a trail of blood from the kitchen into the room where Martha lay. The constable was sure that Allott was the killer.

Allott was arrested and taken to a cell; Boler noticed more blood on the man; on his chin and on his shirt. The constable was very thorough and went back to the farm the next day; there he found a footprint at the end of the garden, and the front of the print pointed towards Allott's farmhouse. He also found an apron which had clearly been used for wiping blood off of something.

At the inquest and the following hearing at a petty sessions court, there were depositions against Allott; he was charged with murder and committed to York. Baron Alderson heard the case, and matters were so clear-cut that the jury did not even need to retire to discuss them: Allott was sentenced to hang. But in those days, constables were clearly not as meticulous as they are today in checking prisoners' belongings and clothes, for Allott was found to have a large knife on him in his cell and was planning to take his own life. He was prevented from doing so, and on 6 April 1835 he was hanged alongside Ursula Lofthouse and Joseph Heeley, of whom we know nothing except that Heeley was a robber. All three prayed loudly before they dropped into the space of death; and the men were buried in the castle grounds.

Lofthouse, who had poisoned her husband, was the last woman to be publicly hanged in Yorkshire. The unpredictable hangman William Curry was in good form that day; he hanged the men first and then gave Ursula as quick a death as was possible. Her body was taken for dissection.

66

SOLDIER IN A RAGE

Charles Batty, 2 April 1836

Charles Batty, an ex-soldier, and his lover, Elizabeth Brown, lived together in Mill Sands; such was their dissolute life that by September 1835, they were faced with the prospect of starvation. A demand for food and a quarrel about a candle then led to Batty going into a violent rage and he attacked her brutally.

Poor Elizabeth was dragged across the room as she screamed for help, and then after she ran away, he grabbed her and threw her down the stairs. The fight was so loud and vicious that people in the street were aware of it, and one man came running to see what was wrong. Elizabeth was found on the floor with her throat cut. Batty was also wounded, but it was clear that he was the attacker and a constable was called. Batty said that he should have finished her long ago, and that she had pawned his clothes. Then the constable arrived and other locals helped to search for evidence; a razor was found and Batty admitted that he had used it to attack her.

But Elizabeth was not yet dead; she sat in a chair with towels pressed to her neck; other wounds were found in various parts of her body. A surgeon worked hard to save her, and she survived, being able to watch Batty stand trial at York. Attempted murder was still a capital offence at that time, so he stood trial for his life.

Baron Parke, presiding, naturally wanted a consideration of possible insanity, and there was no lawyer working for Batty. But he was satisfied from Elizabeth's answers that Batty was not deranged at that time. He had, in fact, threatened to hurt her on several previous occasions. Batty told a tale of her leeching him for money and her sheer intolerable drunkenness; he claimed that she had said to him: 'I'll make you sup sorrow by the spoonful. You shall be hanged or transported for my sake . . .' It then emerged that he had spent all that day drinking, mixing ale and rum. But the constable insisted that Batty was sober when he had been called to the scene. There were no reasons that would condone a planned and brutal attempted murder, and Batty had to die. He was controlled and silent on the scaffold, and died on 2 April 1836.

67

WORKMEN IN MURDEROUS ENCOUNTER

Thomas Williams, 12 August 1837

This is another story of heavy drinking and the fall of a workman into oblivion and serious crime. Thomas Williams was a basket maker working in Sheffield for a man named Moore. The employer was too tolerant of Williams' time off for drinking and on Friday 17 March 1837, after Moore had sacked him and taken on a man named Froggatt, the drink led to murderous thoughts.

Williams went to a public house with a drinking companion, and from there he went across to the workshop to fetch his tools. He saw Froggatt, a man he had vowed to kill, sitting with his back to him. There was an instantaneous drive to attack the man, and Williams took a bill-hook and slammed it on Froggatt's head. He was then heard to say, 'Damn him, I will finish him!' He hit him again, and a workman came into the area to see Froggatt lying on the floor, blood flowing from his head. Some men lifted him onto a cart and took him to the infirmary; he had deep cuts, so severe that his skull was visible.

A constable tracked Williams down easily and there was ample evidence of what Williams had said on that occasion. He said, 'I care nothing for myself, but if I have not killed him and am to suffer for it, I shall be sorry.' But it was a murder case, as the victim died three weeks later.

Depositions were given and heard in the hospital before Froggatt's death, and then there was a post-mortem, at which it was found that Williams had fractured the man's skull in two places and that the brain had been damaged. It was a simple matter at the inquest to return a verdict of wilful murder against Williams and he was destined for York. The usual defence of insanity while drunk was attempted; the line of thought was that insanity had been irritated by drink – in other words, a condition of insanity could be shown to exist. The argument did not work and Williams was sentenced to hang.

Williams prayed at length before he died and incorporated a diatribe on the perils of drunkenness; he left a widow and five children to fight for survival without him. He was buried in the prison grounds.

68

ANOTHER WIFE MURDER

Robert Nall, 9 April 1842

Robert Nall had given his wife Mary years of sheer hell before they parted, and even then he would not leave her alone. His demands turned to frustration and then to violence and he was heard to say to her, 'Thou must prepare thyself for a coffin tomorrow morning for I mean to stick thee.' He took rather longer than he at first said, but later expressed his resolve again, saying he would have a free ride to York. But they were back together again two months later.

In late November, they spent a night together at the Hull Beer House in Sheffield's Wicker district. They then moved on to his sister's house, where they persuaded her to let them stay, as they were drifting around until they could live with her mother – something that was not likely to happen. Nall's sister returned from a visit to find that her brother was uneasy and in a strange mood. Later, having become increasingly worried, she brought a watchman to the house and the two of them found Nall in bed with Mary – but the woman was dead. She was covered in blood, and Nall produced a knife, which he gave to the watchman.

The watchman, Macklin, made a careful note of what Nall said after that. The man said that he had tried to stab and to hang himself, but had not had the resolve to do it. When questioned further, Nall told a story of how, when they were together and drunk, they had argued and Mary had said that she would, 'go with who she liked when she liked.' That provoked him into stabbing her. He had taken her life and then lay with her as she died, waiting for retribution. At the inquest, the coroner said that he had never known a more deliberate act of murder, and Nall was sent to York for that 'free ride' he had spoken of.

Mr Justice Coltman heard that familiar plea of insanity yet again; the argument was that an industrial accident, which had happened some time before, had left Nall with a mental derangement. A surgeon gave supporting evidence, but to no avail. There was no possibility of manslaughter and no provocation. After half an hour, the jury found Nall guilty of murder but did recommend mercy; however, nothing changed the judge's mind that Nall should hang. He said to Nall, 'The state of mind you were in was not such as legally to extenuate your crime. You were responsible for your acts . . . and you must suffer for it.' Nall hanged alongside another wife-killer, Jonathan Taylor.

69

MURDER OF A CHILD

John Rodda, 13 August 1846

On 19 April 1846, John Rodda murdered his only child at Skipton. He had been alone with the baby for just half an hour and it was then rushed to hospital. The child died three days later. The facts are startling and repulsive: he killed the child with oil of vitriol, his motive being to get 50s from a burial club. John Rodda was Irish, and just thirty-three years old; he confessed his guilt to his priest. Burial clubs, like life insurance schemes at that time, presented a tempting way to acquire considerable wealth for the working class. In Rodda's case, the killing provided, at one stroke, the answer to his personal problems and also offered him cash.

The Times reported his last hours with a sense of high drama: 'At an early hour this morning he was removed from his cell to the apartment near the drop and he has been attended by the clergy of the Roman Catholic Church. We are given to understand that he has confessed his guilt and he has died in a state of penitence.' At around midday on 13 August 1846, while a crowd of about a thousand people waited to see Rodda die, the procession of criminal, hangman, staff and priests arrived. The Revd Billington fell to his knees to pray and Rodda joined him.

70

THE MURDER OF ESTHER INMAN

Thomas Malkin, 6 January 1849

At a restaurant in Vicar Lane, Leeds, two days after cutting the throat of his sweetheart, Esther Inman, seventeen-year-old Thomas Malkin was apprehended. He was charged with her murder and kept on remand until the coroner's court could sit with some medical information to hand. Esther's body was identified by her stepfather who testified that he had seen two people at the bottom of his garden on the night of the murder, but could not make out who they were.

When he heard Esther's voice entreat, 'Father, open the door!' he realised who it was and did so. But he then saw that she was lying on her back in the garden and he went out to her. Thomas Inman brought her inside and saw immediately that she was bleeding profusely from her chest, on the right side. She died soon after being taken inside. She was just sixteen and the surgeon who arrived, within ten minutes, was too late to save her. Mary Ann Umpleby gave evidence, saying that Esther and Malkin had been very close and she knew Malkin; on the night of the murder she had seen him running in the clear moonlight in the direction away from the garden. She had seen Esther and Malkin together earlier.

Esther had told a girl named Mary Ann Smith that she did not want to continue her friendship with Malkin and that earlier on the day of the murder she had been out to Kirkstall without him. When they had been seen together, it was on occasions when the girl was trying to tell him that she wanted to see him no more. But the young man's intentions were confirmed when a blacksmith said that Malkin had asked him to make a special blade for him; it was, the man said, 'about eight inches long and a quarter of an inch thick'. Another craftsman said he had filed a bevelled edge on the blade.

When arrested by Inspector Childs, Malkin claimed he did not know his name and had no recollection of the murder. But he had plunged the special blade into Esther's chest; the surgeon said that it had penetrated to a depth of about 2½in, so it was used with considerable force. Wilful murder was returned against Malkin; he simply said, 'Well sir, I have nothing to say . . . I don't know anything about the murder.'

Malkin was sent for trial to York, found guilty and sentenced to hang. On the day of his execution, a local report noted that, 'The influx of strangers from Hunslet and other parts of the West Riding was very great . . . they had been walking all night.' As Malkin walked onto the scaffold with the Revd Sutton and they began to pray, there were 12,000 people present. It was a rare event at that time to see a teenager hanged.

71

REPRIEVE APPEALS FAIL

William Ross, 19 August 1850

William Ross murdered his wife and almost escaped the gallows; on 9 August 1850, he was granted a week's respite by Sir George Grey so that various written statements about the case could be more closely examined. An investigation took place at the White Hart public house at Saddleworth, led by three magistrates; Buckley, Whitehead and Robinson. There was more drama in this than in the circumstances of the murder, mainly because the Secretary of State had requested that certain people should be examined, along with requests made by Ross's own solicitor.

Ross had been convicted of killing his wife, Mary. She had been poisoned, but he maintained that he had bought some poison at Ashton, buying it for a woman named Martha Backley. When he was found guilty, he heard the sentence of death with great firmness, and when asked if he had anything to say, replied, 'I am not guilty, my Lord. I am not guilty of the crime.' But he had an active and determined legal counsel and the requests for reprieves began. However, finally, on the morning of the Friday after his short respite, the gaoler at York received news that the sentence stood and that the execution must take its course.

We know a great deal about Ross's last days. The reports even tell us that he was 'greatly debilitated by diarrhoea' and that he also had epileptic fits; he had had these fits previously, while this was at a time when little was known about that illness. We know that, as *The Times* added, 'Up to the last few moments of his life . . . and in the most solemn manner, he declared his innocence to his spiritual adviser, the rev. the ordinary of the castle.' When the day came for his hanging, we also have plenty of incidental detail: there were only a few persons gathered to watch until within just half an hour of the appointed time; then a crowd of almost 4,000 people assembled. Ross met his fate, the chaplain at his side, with resolve and acceptance; but after the usual one hour of hanging after death, the unusual measure was taken of making a cast of his skull. After all, this was the age of phrenology, and some experts wanted to relate evil to bumps on the head. Ross, innocent or not, would live on, at least as a specimen in some northern laboratory.

72

GREAT COOLNESS OF CONDUCT

Alfred Waddington, 8 January 1853

Young Sarah Slater, pregnant with Alfred Waddington's child, knew he was a tearaway with a robbery in his dark history; but he asked her to marry him. She asked for sureties that they would have a stable married life; on his part, he was suspicious that she had another man – a wealthy one, and so jealousy grew in his mind.

When the child was born, the usual process of affiliation order and the threat of gaol loomed for Waddington. He became violent. After letting his payments slip, he received a summons; his response was to threaten and intimidate Sarah. Later, when a young girl took the little child for a walk, Waddington appeared; he snatched the child and ran off with it. A frantic and wild series of events then took place, with Waddington telling Sarah that the child had fallen off a wall, and then that he would murder it. His words were, 'Thou can either save thy child's life or kill it.' But things escalated into open assault and he slashed at Sarah with a knife, cutting the back of her neck; she was saved by a boy in the streets after shouting 'Murder!' and managed to run to her mother's house.

There was still a search on for the missing child. Waddington even cut the face of one of Sarah's friends. He was now the centre of a reign of terror in the streets. By that night, Waddington went to a watchman and gave himself up, saying he had cut off his child's head. This was true, as police officers discovered when they went to Cutler's Wood at Heeley and found the body of the child; its head was indeed severed from the body. Waddington was taken to the chief of police, and then the prisoner ranted about Sarah becoming 'a rich man's whore'. Two days later the young man stood in front of the magistrate and the mayor; he was remanded until the inquest and at that hearing, the corpse of the child was actually brought into the court, and it is recorded that Waddington turned away and covered his face as a distraught Sarah screamed and asked the assembled public, ' Oh! Is he not a villain?'

Waddington was committed to York where Mr Justice Talfourd heard the case. Talfourd was not sympathetic to the notion of capital punishment, but on this occasion he had a lengthy defence argument to hear – one of insanity, naturally. The reasoning in the defence was complex and clever. It raised issues of sanity and its definition, but in the end it was clear that there had been an intention to kill. In his summing-up, Talfourd said: 'The question for the jury is whether or not at the time of the crime the prisoner was afflicted with a mental disease which prevented him from knowing and understanding the nature of the act which he committed . . .'

The jury had no doubt that Waddington intended to take the child's life and that he knew what he was doing. Talfourd commented on Waddington's 'great coolness of conduct' and was clearly upset as he passed the death sentence; his only mention of a pardon was in relation to that from the young man's maker. Waddington was hanged on 8 January 1853; James Barbour, a man who had killed his wife, was granted a short reprieve and was executed a week later. As for Waddington, a crowd of 8,000 Sheffielders watched him hang. He was just twenty, and had a mercifully quick death.

Master Serjeant Talfourd, from a portrait collection, 1840.

73

GUILTY OF TAKING A
WOMAN'S LIFE

John Hannah, 27 September 1856

On Christmas Eve 1856, a letter appeared in the *Leeds Mercury* signed by various people to the effect that John Hannah, awaiting execution at York, should have his sentence commuted to life imprisonment. The letter presents a list of instances suggesting that Hannah had been suffering from mental illness at the time of the murder of his live-in partner, Jane Banham. The letter gives instances of a 'glassy-eyed stare' Hannah had had at the time. It stresses that he and Banham had had children together, but that she had gone to live in Halifax, and he had begged her to come back to him.

The instance of the murder was described by the newspaper in this way: 'On the 11th of September he obtained an interview with the deceased at the Malt Mill Inn at Armley. He again urged her to return to him and was flippantly refused. In a short time persons in the house heard a scuffle in the room where prisoner and the deceased were together, and on entering, found him in the act of cutting her throat . . .' It seems that Hannah had no idea what he had done and was mentally deranged. Other witnesses said he mumbled in his talk and had tried to hurt himself while in custody. He was a working tailor, and such men always carried a razor, and so was not, the letter implied, carrying it with the express purpose of taking Jane's life.

The letter's writer had also contacted a man who stayed in the same lodgings as Hannah, and described his agitated state, sleeplessness and worry about the children as he lived apart from Jane. Hannah himself petitioned the Queen for a pardon, describing his army record – that he had served in the Royal Artillery for twenty years and had fought at Flushing, and afterwards been in Wellington's army.

All this was for nothing. He was hanged before several thousand people on 27 December 1856. He had constantly said that he did not premeditate the murder. He wrote letters to his parents, and then quoted a poem for his mother:

Light is the turf of my tomb
may its verdure like emeralds be
there should not be a shadow of gloom
in ought that remains of me.

Hannah died with a prayer-book in his hands, but it was a slow and agonising death. Every stage in the narrative of this case testifies to the increasing difficulties the criminal justice system had by the mid-Victorian period in coping with the complexities of the notion of insanity and its relation to the concept of premeditation in homicides.

74

THE WADSWORTH MOOR MURDER

Joseph Shepherd, 3 April 1858

The body of Bethel Parkinson, a young farmer, was found on the lower mowing-field of Commons Farm, Wadsworth Moor. His head, neck and face were covered in blood, and there were severe wounds on his face. Bethel had been seen with Joseph Shepherd by various people, most noticeably in the context of their discussing money-making schemes. Bethel's widow, Mary, spoke to the local constable, saying that they lived at the time at Raggald's Inn at Thornton, and she explained that Bethel mainly dealt in cattle. She had seen Shepherd with her husband earlier on the day of the killing.

At the inquest at the White Horse Inn, Hebden Bridge, Shepherd was reported to be in 'worse spirits than before, more aware of his awful position.' A stack of circumstantial evidence was against him, including a man who saw him with a knife that matched one found close to the body. There was also a stone with blood marks on it, taken from a wall near the murder scene, and this formed part of the evidence. Shepherd had also tried to sell the knife, which had been recalled by the proprietor of the shop.

A verdict of wilful murder was returned; police staff had given accounts of cuts on the body of Shepherd, tears in his coat and bloodstains which had been only partially sponged off. Even Shepherd's father did not help the cause by talking openly about his knives, and how one was unaccountably missing. The motive was money – Bethel had done a deal and Shepherd was hard up. All these details put together meant that Shepherd was bound for York, and at the Assizes the information was all repeated, and this time the noose was waiting for him when the returned verdict was guilty.

Shepherd was only twenty-two. His wife and father came to visit him in the condemned cell; his father tried repeatedly to have more time with his son, but his request to speak to him on the morning of the execution was turned down, as was proper according to protocol then. The Maltby hangman, Thomas Askern, officiated at the execution. He did an unusually professional job on that occasion, hanging a young man who had resisted all religious consolation during his period in the death cell.

75

THE SHEPHERD SWEETHEART

John Taylor Whitworth, 8 January 1859

John Taylor Whitworth was twenty-two, an assistant shepherd working for a Mr Machin at Gateford. This was around five miles from the home of Sally Hare, and the two became sweethearts.

On 30 September 1858, Whitworth went to visit Sally while her parents were out. They talked and ate some supper, then, as they sat by the fire, he began making advances towards her. He pushed himself on her but she refused and he left the house in a bad mood. But he persuaded her to walk with him.

That was a fatal decision; he was still enraged and spiralling out of control. As they walked in the dark at a place called Throapham Common, he tried again to seduce her. After that, he became irrational and accused her of having another man. He said that they should die together taking poison: the gist of his reasoning was that if he could not have her, then no one else would. When Sally dismissed this as nonsense, he turned violent and threatened to kill her. A report at the time tells us what happened: 'He took hold of her, threw her down on the ground. Placed his knee upon her, pulled out his pocket-knife, opened it and stabbed her in the neck, the blade penetrating to the bone.' But Sally was a woman of spirit and considerable strength. She fought him like a demon and managed to grab Whitworth's hair; then she took the knife from his hand and threw him down onto the earth. She ran home and told the tale, but was bleeding severely and although a surgeon was called, after a few days, she died.

Whitworth was arrested and he had a cut on his throat. He fabricated a tale about them both fighting for the knife; but the poor girl, in her dying declaration, told the account as we have it here. The outcome was clear: it was a case of murder. Before Mr Baron Watson, he was sentenced to hang. Whitworth was alone in the death cell, receiving no visitors. He was penitent; there had been no appeals, nor attempts on behalf of the defense to claim insanity. On the morning of the hanging, a Saturday, a crowd had gathered and most were quiet but for a few loud voices calling out, 'Bring out Atkinson!' This was a reference to a man who had committed a similar killing at Darley, but had been reprieved. There was no reprieve for Whitworth: he came outside after taking Holy Communion, was silent while he prepared for death and when he was hanged, he struggled on the end of the rope for two minutes and then his body was buried in the grounds of the castle.

76

THE KILLING OF ALICE RILEY

John Riley, 6 August 1859

In Mariner's Court, Blackfriargate, Hull, John Riley and his wife, Alice, lived in a one-room lodging house. They had a turbulent marriage, having first lived in Lincolnshire, and then had a serious argument which led to John taking a knife to Alice and threatening her. Alice quite justifiably left him and went over the Humber to live well away from him, but he began to make overtures to patch things up and before long they were together again, though living in poverty.

From this point on, the disreputable man's life degenerates: he did no work but lived off his wife's earnings as a seamstress. When that did not earn enough for his wants, he put her on the streets to bring in money from selling her body. Not surprisingly, she took to drink. They quarrelled often and loudly; it was a natural outcome of this that violence emerged, and Alice was the victim. He took her life and, as one lawyer commented: 'The man seemed to have been tired of this world, and so he determined to take her life, and then planned committing suicide himself.'

Riley had assaulted her some time before and had spent a term in prison; the defence counsel tried to claim that he had learned from this and that they had lived fairly well together for some time before the latest and final furore in the house. The question for the jury was to decide whether Riley had planned this murder or whether in the heat of a quarrel, he reached for a weapon and took his wife's life. They decided it was murder, and as the judge spoke the death sentence, he added, 'Your days are numbered – the days you have to pass in this world are few and I exhort you to make good use of your time . . . Sue for that mercy and pardon that is denied you in this world.'

John Riley was hanged on 6 August 1859, a man indeed 'tired of this world'.

77

KILLED FOR A WATCH

Charles Normington, 31 December 1859

Charles Normington was just eighteen years of age when he murdered a man named Broughton in Leeds. Normington was illiterate and a drifter. On the day of the murder he had seen Broughton out walking on a route from Roundhay into Leeds centre. In 1859 Harehills Lane was mainly rural. The fields there were a pleasant place to walk, and Richard Broughton walked there, without much on him that would attract a robber, but he was set upon my Normington and another man. The victim was an old man, but he managed to recover and stagger to his feet; then he was helped homewards. But he was mortally injured; a doctor was called and police went to the scene of the crime.

Broughton died soon after, so a murder hunt was on. The victim gave a description before he died and two suspects were found, but they each had a sound alibi. The search extended to Castleford, where a man named Smales had bought a pawn ticket for a watch, and this enquiry led to Normington. He was arrested in Sheffield, and he claimed that he was just an accessory as another man had actually killed the old man, but there were bloodstains on one of his shirts. He was charged with murder and sentenced.

In court, his mother screamed out in shock; after that, as he was in the condemned cell, the illiterate teenager had to dictate letters home to a scribe, and in one of these he said, 'I put all my trust in the Lord Jesus Christ . . . I have quite resigned myself, and do not dread the hour so fast approaching.'

On the day of his death, Normington was not able to eat breakfast; and then he was changed into the clothes in which he would die – a white harding labourer's jacket and corduroy trousers. Then, at seven o'clock he was escorted to a room next to the scaffold. There he knelt on the drop while the chaplain read the funeral service and then shook hands with him. As he fell he shouted, 'Lord have mercy on me!' and then was convulsed for a few minutes, with his knees jerked up to his body.

78

HAWKSWORTH HALL GAMEKEEPER SHOT DEAD

James Waller, 4 January 1862

This case is arguably one of the most notorious murders in Bingley's history, being a revenge killing and involving the age-old enmity of gamekeepers and poachers. James Waller, a thirty-one-year-old woolcomber chose Bonfire Night 1861 as the time he would exact revenge on William Smith, gamekeeper of Hawksworth Hall, a man who had annoyed Waller so much in the past that his day of reckoning had finally arrived.

Waller approached his victim in the evening with a double-barrelled shotgun. He turned, having been seen, and let the gamekeeper give chase, then stopped, turned and fired. Smith put his hand to his chest and said that he was done for. Then Waller shot him in the chest again. This was a most uncomplicated crime, with no attempt to cover things up or be in any way subtle. Several people were around and they approached the spot where they had heard the shots. It took Smith (who was known locally as Davey) a long time to die. There was soon a police hunt in action, searching for Waller. There were no other suspects.

The inquest was held at the Angel Inn, Baildon, and the jury were taken to see the corpse of the victim. An officer from Otley, Sergeant Inman, said that he had heard Waller say he would blow Smith's brains out. Waller had always been rash, reckless and outspoken. Surely the most interesting witness was Ann Wilkinson. Waller had simply walked into her home, openly saying he wanted a good place from which to see and shoot his victim. It was just a case of *when* the police would track him down – not *if* they would. They found Waller in a barn and he was said to be 'pale and haggard and much reduced.'

Waller pleaded not guilty at the trial at York but that meant nothing. The facts were clear; the motive was well known and the evidence was substantial. There were several reliable witnesses. He was condemned to hang and a large crowd turned out to watch him die. When his neck was stretched, almost 10,000 people were there to witness it. It took him ten minutes to die – a horribly inhumane statistic in the history of York executions. His last words were that he hoped there was no bad feeling between him and Smith when they met in the next world.

THE LAST PUBLIC EXECUTION IN THE CITY

Frederick Parker, 4 April 1868

Daniel Driscoll was a journeyman bricklayer who lived with his mother in Tottenham, but he took to the road to find work and finally he ended up in Beverley. He was committed to the House of Correction there and was released on 29 February 1868. When he came out of that prison, he left with another criminal, Frederick Parker, a Hemingbrough man who had done two months inside. Driscoll had a little money on him – over £4 – and he also had a watch and silver chain.

The men stayed together and started a pub crawl that took them from Beverley to Bubwith, and then towards Hemingbrough. Bubwith was where Driscoll was last seen alive. His body was later found near South Duffield, his head badly wounded, and it was clear to those who found him that a hedge-stake had been used to kill him. Driscoll had also been robbed of his

The Beverley House of Correction. (Author's collection)

watch and chain. Some of the clothing belonging to the dead man was examined by a Dr Proctor at York, and blood was found on the waistcoat and trousers.

Parker had had a varied and eventful life: he had been taken in by his uncle after his father's death and had been a young villain, sentenced to a spell inside for attempting to upset a train on the Market Weighton and Selby line. After stealing cloth and being sent to the Wakefield House of Correction, he joined the Pontefract Militia. At his death, he was just twenty-one, and a final irony was that, as he had just killed a man for a few pounds, there was a legacy due to him worth £21. There was a rumour in his home town that he had assaulted another young man some months before, hitting him on the head with a stick. Of course, Parker denied this.

Parker was found guilty and indeed confessed his guilt. The reports on him were, as usual, concerned with repentance and salvation, and the reporter for the *Hull Packet* gave a series of minute details of the ritual, including the fact that, as Parker knelt down, the hangman wore a white waistcoat and that for the first time the railing around the scaffold was draped with black cloth, and so when the drop fell, the crowd were screened away from a view of the dying agonies of the culprit.

That year, 1868, was to be the last in which the British public were able to watch a hanging. After that, executions were conducted within the walls of the gaols.

80

HE TOOK HIS SISTER'S LIFE

William Jackson, 18 August 1874

William Jackson was described as a 'fine looking man, only twenty-nine years of age and of military bearing, had for several years served in the 77th Foot, and afterwards in the army reserve.' This is all very admirable, but it was written about him just after he was hanged at York on 18 August 1874. He came back from service abroad to live with his parents, but there were constant quarrels and he had a serious drinking problem.

The drunk became a killer one night after he left home to go to Ripon and meet his sister. Her body was found the next day, with the throat cut. Jackson had been seen with her and then went missing, so the hunt for him began; he was found near Bishop Auckland. Near the body of his sister a pipe was found with blood on it and a razor case. Jackson admitted knowledge of the murder when arrested and questioned. He was tried and found guilty of murder, and it is recorded that he insisted that he was innocent from that time until he was sentenced to die. But in his last hours Jackson wrote a full confession, and the account he gave is as follows:

> My sister went with me until we got to the other end of the barn field . . . She said, 'No, I'll go with you now, for when you go away you never write.' . . . When she got up to me I turned and said, 'Now Lizzie, you had better go back.' She says to me, 'I will not go back, wherever thou goes I will go with thee.' So I made no more to do, I opened my black bag and took out my razor and I cut my sister's throat.

He also said that he loved her dearer than himself, and that he was sorry for not having confessed 'that great sin' earlier.

The hangman, Askern, came with the two county sheriffs on the morning of the execution and Jackson was pinioned. He walked, according to a witness, 'with a firm step' but it was

A depiction of a hanging scene. (Illustrated Police News, 1867)

a botched job and his death was slow and painful. The witness wrote 'The twitching of the nerves and the spasmodic movements of the body could be seen for fully three minutes after the bolt had been drawn.' Jackson had knelt down and joined in the holy service as the bells of St Mary's tolled. But to this day, his reason for undertaking such a drastic method of putting an end to the irritations of his beloved sister remain a mystery and must lie in some kind of mental derangement in him.

81

A BOTCHED EXECUTION

Vincent Walker, 15 April 1878

In February 1878, a reporter from Hull gave an account of one of the most brutal killings in the city's history. As the writer pointed out, the last three murders in Hull had taken place within a one mile radius of this one. The victim was Lydia Walker, whose husband, Vincent, was enraged that she was spending time at a Mrs White's house; in fact he went there with an axe in his hand, ready to create mayhem.

Walker arrived at Mrs White's house and asked where his wife was. When told she was upstairs 'with a gentleman', Walker lunged a blade at Mrs White and then went on the rampage. The landlady was stabbed over thirty times, such was the frenzy of this killer. People heard the noise and came to help, but Walker had gone outside and then he stopped another woman walking past, grabbed her and said, 'Does anyone else want a dose?' A neighbour, Mrs Rogers, was caught up in all this and tried her best to help. A hue and cry was raised and a crowd gathered, as Walker ran outside and threw his knife away. He had not used the axe, or there could have been much more injury done.

The attacker was seized by a group of men and taken to a constable; this officer unwisely took his prisoner back to the house where Mrs White lay dying to be sure of what had happened; Walker tried to kick the dying woman then. The clasp knife Walker had thrown away was collected by a man and given to the constable. When the inquest took place, there were plenty of witnesses and all kinds of evidence stacked against Walker. Mrs White had died and the jury had been to view her body. There was an adjournment until medical testimony could be given, but soon Walker was in front of the magistrates and the police constable stated that Walker had said he had done the killing wilfully. He added, 'I am very sorry my bitch was not there so I could have given her the same dose.' He was committed to York, and there he was tried and sentenced to die.

His executioner was the celebrated William Marwood, a Lincolnshire man who had devised the more humane 'long drop' hanging method which aimed at killing by asphyxiation rather than by rough strangulation. But this was destined to be one of his few botched jobs. The reporter for the *Hull Packet* noted that Marwood 'deftly tied the prisoner's legs, and during this operation the prisoner's fortitude seemed rather to desert him, for he moaned many times.' The worst was yet to come. The same writer noted, 'The drop allowed for was between five and six feet and the poor fellow suffered awhile, for fully seven minutes elapsed from the bolt being withdrawn to the time when the rope ceased to vibrate.' The body was then cut down and the black flag was raised.

William Marwood, a regular visitor to officiate at the gallows. (Laura Carter)

THE KILLING OF THE OULTON GAMEKEEPER

John D'Arcy, 17 May 1879

John D'Arcy, an Irishman, was only twenty-seven when he was hanged at York, but he had already served seven years' penal servitude at the notorious Spike Island Prison, after being sentenced at the Leitrim Assizes for breaking into a Roman Catholic chapel. Not long after being released, he made his way to Leeds and was clearly a dangerous character, as he was under surveillance, being obliged to report to the police regularly while he was in Yorkshire.

D'Arcy was working as a travelling watchmaker when he came across William Metcalfe, an old man who was the gamekeeper and lodge-keeper at Oulton Park. Some women heard

Illustration of Charlie Peace's arrest, 1880, an influence on this killer. (Author's collection)

a cry come from that lodge and saw that the old man was being robbed and attacked. A man named Mosely came to help and took hold of the outside door in an attempt to prevent the intruder leaving, but D'Arcy was a desperate man and had a gun. Referring to the notorious villain, Charlie Peace, he shouted, 'There'll be another Peace case if you don't release the door!' Peace had been hanged at Armley Gaol just two months previously, and his fame spread in all the true crime publications, giving him some dark glamour among the tougher criminals. D'Arcy got his way and ran off, leaving Metcalfe battered to death.

D'Arcy was caught after information was given by his niece, and police tracked him down to Hunslet. He was committed to York, and at the trial there was no shortage of witnesses for identification and testimony regarding his attack and murder. There was an abundance of circumstantial evidence, and D'Arcy was sentenced to hang. He recieved no visitors in York and never made a confession. William Marwood officiated again, and this time was in control of the system. A reporter from *The Times* witnessed the scene and wrote: 'The condemned man never lost his nerve, and walked with the utmost coolness to the gallows . . . Father Fryer stepped up and asked if he had anything to say. D'Arcy replied that he was innocent . . . The bolt was then drawn and the culprit died without a struggle.'

83

BATTERED TO DEATH WITH A STAKE

John Wood, 11 May 1880

The humble hedge-stake has been a common murder weapon through the ages, since land was enclosed, and it has appeared several times in these chronicles. In this case, it was the implement that killed John Coe. On 27 February 1880, The *Leeds Mercury* reported that the hunt was on for John Wood: 'A strong body of police have been scouring the country round since Monday but they have not yet succeeded in apprehending Wood, although it is firmly believed he is hiding in the locality.' Coe's body had been found on 16 February – he had been battered by a hedge-stake. Beside his body was a piece of branch people had seen Wood carrying.

The two men had been drinking together at a public house in Rotherham called the Chequers Inn and at other drinking-houses. Plenty of passers-by saw them together around the town, mainly at Westgate and in the High Street. The hunt for the killer succeeded when he tried to sell a watch that had belonged to Coe, and there was a report that he had told one of his friends about the Coe murder before anyone could have known.

At York he stood before Mr Justice Stephens. It was a clear-cut case with no shortage of evidence. Within a week he was in the condemned cell, and as usual, the *Hull Packet* was full of macabre detail about the man's last days and death. The press men were admitted inside and escorted by the sheriff's staff, and then a reporter noted that there were two cells close to the scaffold, and in one of them, Wood lay, waiting for the end. We have an account of the arrangements for hanging here: 'It is a permanent scaffold which is raised and blocks up the passage under ordinary circumstances. But yesterday it had been let down and formed the hideous arrangement of the modern gallows . . .'

Wood received no letter from home, as he had been hoping that his parents would write, but no post arrived; he asked a warder to write a letter for him and he was also allowed to write to a friend. Then, before he was hanged, he was asked to speak but said nothing. The report in the *Hull Packet* adds, 'He uttered not a word and took no part in the chaplain's service. His fall on the scaffold was nearly nine feet and he appeared to die instantly.' William Marwood was back to his reliable, professional self, applying his long drop to good effect.

84

A KILLING AT SEA

Edward Wheatfall, 28 November 1882

Edward Wheatfall worked as a second hand on a fishing smack called the *Gleamor*, and at sea on 24 February, he went to see a teenager named Peter Hughes, got him out of his bunk and told him to work with some ropes. Hughes was actually working as the cook but he was being victimised by the violent Wheatfall. The poor young man had been the subject of beatings and torture since the boat left Hull. At one point, Wheatfall shut the boy in the ice-room with no clothes on.

The older man had made it clear from the start of the voyage that he was going to make Hughes' life hell. On 23 February, it was later reported, he kicked the boy so savagely that the lad cried out, 'Oh kill me at once, I can't bear this any longer!' A few days later, after more beatings, he took the boy and after an assault, the lad went overboard, either by suicide or thrown over – the details are unclear. At court, as there was no body and therefore the possibility that Hughes might still be alive, there was a case for the defence, but the jury found Wheatfall guilty of murder. The killer had a long record of crimes and was well known to the Hull police as a thug and a bully.

William Marwood was again in York and he pinioned the seaman in his cell; the condemned man then walked 'with firmness' to the scaffold. The drop was long and the death quick; the reporter who witnessed the death wrote that, 'Throughout, the wretched man submitted to the preparations for executions in the most unconcerned manner, and from first to last uttered not a single word . . .'

85

THE BARNSLEY MURDERER

James Murphy, 29 November 1886

We know a lot about the last days of James Murphy in York before he was hanged, because the hangman, James Berry, kept a journal and published his memoirs. Murphy even managed to joke about his impending death.

Murphy, from Barnsley, was a collier at Lambert's Fold, Dodsworth, and he had twenty-five convictions for poaching. Full of vengeance, Murphy set out one day to look for a police officer named Austwick, and he shot the man dead. He was cornered and arrested in Barnsley, but there was a local groundswell of feeling that he did not deserve to be hanged, as it was thought that the crime was done on the spur of the moment, and not premeditated. An appeal for a reprieve failed.

When Berry came to have his chat in the condemned cell, Murphy said he would not give the hangman any trouble: 'I am not afraid to die. A lot of people have been making a fuss about me. But I'm hanged if I can see what there is to make a fuss about.' Berry was impressed by the sick joke. Murphy had to walk past his own waiting grave on the way to the scaffold, and all he said to Berry was that he wanted him to do it 'as painlessly as you can'.

Berry's note in his journal was, 'I hanged James Murphy in spite of threats and then I heard that I would never dare set foot in Barnsley, the town whence the victim hailed. People said that the Barnsley miners would murder me, but in spite of the threats I visited the town on many occasions.' Usually, Berry was happy to enjoy his notoriety and the fact that the media took an interest in him. In Leeds, the printer Charles Johnson produced a biography of Murphy in a chapbook, with the title, *The Life of James Murphy, the Barnsley Murderer*, and it meant that the killer would be the first name linked to the town in that way. The picture of Murphy on the cover of the book shows a calm, ordinary man with arms folded, as if waiting for a conversation about the weather.

Life of James Murphy, *from a chapbook, 1890.* (Author's collection)

86

MURDER OF A CONSTABLE

Robert Kitching, 30 December 1890

In September 1890, Sergeant James Weedy saw a horse and cart tied up outside the Leeming Bar Hotel. Being an efficient village constable, he wasted no time telling the owner, Robert Kitching, to move the vehicle. That should have been the end of the matter, but Kitching was in the mood for a fight. He told the officer that he would bide his time and move the cart when he was ready. Obviously, the officer could not back down. He insisted that the cart be moved.

Before he stormed out, market gardener Kitching said, with plenty of witnesses to hear him, that he would blow the sergeant's brains out. Kitching knew Weedy's route on his regular beat and he took his gun and lay in wait for him. Mrs Kitching ran to tell a neighbour but she was too late for any warning to be given; both women heard a gunshot. Kitching went to tell his father-in-law what he had done; they then went to the body, which was just out of sight from the road where it would be found.

As Kitching had publicly told the world about his intention to kill Weedy, he was the man police officers went to find and charge, soon after a huntsman from the Bedale Hunt had found the body. At the York trial, the only claim for the defence was of self-defence but this was pathetically slender and Kitching was found guilty of murder. His hangman was John Billington, and Kitching was apparently silent and penitent, submitting to the pinioning without resistance. For this hanging, we know the men who were in the full procession: Edwin Taylor, the governor; both sheriffs; the chaplain; and the prison surgeon. The report noted that, 'Just as Billington pulled the lever, the condemned man appeared to fall slightly forward although he was in the act of fainting, but this did not appear to interfere with the carrying out of the execution.' Kitching had made a statement to the chaplain that he had killed the officer intentionally.

87

DEAD & BURIED

Robert Hudson, 13 August 1895

Robert Hudson killed his wife and child on Helmsley Moor, stabbing them to death. Their bodies were found buried there and Hudson was tracked down and finally arrested in Birmingham on 22 June 1895, where he confessed to the murder. The family had arrived a few weeks before the horrible event and had taken lodgings in the town in Bondgate. It was reported that for two weeks they lived there as if on holiday and on friendly terms, the three of them often taking rides into the country.

But on 8 June they all left together, yet Hudson returned alone. He told people that his wife and child were staying with an aunt in Hovingham. Later, Mrs Holmes, the landlady,

The arrest of Robert Hudson.
(Illustrated Police News, 1895)

received a note, ostensibly from Mrs Hudson, asking her to forward their clothes to an address in Darlington. Things became more complex after that when Hudson's sister arrived to ask for more of the belongings, and Mrs Holmes learned that Hudson had apparently split from his wife, as she 'had taken off with a Helmsley man', as Mrs Holmes later put it in court. This aroused suspicions and enquiries began, leading to the discovery that Hudson had been lying and so became a wanted man by the police. The bodies were found, their throats having been cut with a large carving knife, and Mrs Hudson's clothing was badly torn.

In the death cell, it was noted that 'all along [Hudson] had shown indifference to his fate' and on the morning of the day he was to die he 'ate a hearty breakfast'. James Billington was Hudson's executioner and the culprit met him with calmness after listening to sermons and supposedly fortifying words from the prison chaplain. Hudson wrote a letter to his parents before he walked out to eternity. In that letter he wrote about mixing with bad company, initially in Nottingham, and then he recounted his fall from order and married life into crime. He had what was then called, 'a dignified death, being the foundation of his hopes for repentance before the judgement of the next world'.

88

A SWEDISH SAILOR HANGS

August Carlsen, 22 December 1896

August Carlsen had no thoughts of Christmas in mind as he sat in the York death cell in 1896. He had just a few days to live, for he had murdered Julia Wood in Hull on 23 July of that year. Carlsen and Wood were lodging in the city with a Mrs McCann, and it was well known among his workmates that he loved Julia and that he gave her money and wrote to her when he was at sea, writing very passionately and fondly to her. But in July, when he came on shore, he and Julia had a long drinking session and it was noticed that they both drank huge quantities of brandy and beer. Early that evening, Carlsen came to his landlady and said, 'I have killed Florrie' (his nickname for Julia).

HORRIBLE TRAGEDY IN YORKSHIRE.

A MOTHER AND CHILD MURDERED.

FOUND BURIED IN THE MOORS.

Helmsley, Sunday.

This morning Helmsley was thrown into a state of great excitement by the discovery that a Mrs Hudson and her child had been murdered and buried on the moors, four miles north of the town. It appears that three weeks ago Robert Hudson, a native of the locality, who was brought up on the moors, came to Helmsley with his wife and child, and took lodgings with Mrs Holmes, of Bondgate. During a fortnight they lived there apparently on friendly terms, and went for long drives ostensibly with the object of seeing the country. Mrs Hudson, however, complained that the places visited were lonely. On June 8th Hudson and his wife and child left their lodgings early in the morning, Hudson returning alone in the afternoon, and stating that his wife and child were staying with an aunt at Hovingham. Hudson further declared they would return on the following Monday, when Mrs Holmes should accompany them for a drive on the moors. The visitors to Helmsley, however, did not return, but Mrs Holmes received a note written in the name of Mrs Hudson in lead pencil asking that clothes ought to be forwarded to Darlington. Mrs Hudson's sister last Friday came to Helmsley from Sheffield with a second letter, also written in lead pencil, this being from Hudson, stating that his wife had gone away and "he was jealous she had taken off with a Helmsley man." Suspicion was then aroused, and the relatives of the deceased made inquiries. Finding that no visit had been paid to Hovingham, a search was made on the moors, which was futile for a long time, but finally a hole was found to have been recently dug near the road. The bodies of Mrs Hudson and her child were there discovered, the soil covering them being only three inches deep. Both the victims were found to have had their throats deeply cut, and a large carving-knife was discovered on the breast of the woman Mrs Hudson's clothing was badly torn. The bodies were conveyed to the mortuary at Helmsley to await the inquest. No arrest has yet been made.

Report on the Hudson case. (*Daily News*, 1895)

When the doctor and a constable arrived they found Carlsen on the bed, his arms around the woman he loved but whom he had killed in a terrible way: he had cut her throat. As the constable talked to him, he said, 'I am willing to die . . . I am ready to die for her any minute.' The *Hull Packet* reported: 'At the trial evidence was called to show that the woman had behaved badly towards Carlsen, and that he was so intoxicated when committing the crime that he had not formed such an intention as is necessary to constitute wilful murder.' But he was found guilty, and the recommendation for mercy was ignored.

Waiting for death, Carlsen was repentant and spent a lot of time with the chaplain; he went to Matins in the prison chapel and then the under-sheriff led him to the scaffold. The reporter who witnessed this pointed out that Carlsen 'made no statement about the crime beyond contending that his mind was a perfect blank as to what occurred on the night of the murder'.

R.E. Triffit, governor of York Prison in the 1890s. (Laura Carter)

CURIOSITIES

Who Hanged William Dove?

One of the most sensational cases and trials in the nineteenth century was that of William Dove, a young man from a Methodist family who was led to kill his wife. At the centre of the scandal was Dove's relationship with Leeds 'wizard' Henry Harrison, a man who was also a quack doctor with a practice in the centre of Leeds. Owen Davies, in his book on the subject, states: 'nearly all the relevant court records are lost. The Assize depositions are missing from the boxes . . . and there are no surviving Leeds coroners' papers from the period.' Yet the incredible story has been reconstructed by Davies.

Dove was hanged at York after a trial at the Summer Assizes in July 1856. But the real interest in terms of this chronicle is the matter of who hanged Dove? We know that he was hanged 'in front of St George's Field' on 9 August 1856, and the line of thought has always been that he was hanged by Thomas Askern, the regular York hangman at the time. But Askern denied this in the press. Askern wrote to several Yorkshire newspapers to claim that he never carried out the execution, yet the official line was that he did do the hanging and that he was paid £5. Askern wrote: 'My impression has always been that great pains were taken by newspaper editors to get accurate information from trustworthy sources, but that impression is altogether obliterated . . .'

But it is hard to escape the fact that a number of people recalled seeing Askern hang Dove. The only puzzling thing about the letters to the papers is that he was so literate and articulate; Askern was a farmer, butcher and cattle-jobber from Maltby and rarely used the written word. In the end, there were no other candidates for the dubious role of hangman to Dove, and so we have no real reason why he was so offended and why he was driven to write so many times denying his role in that sensational case and its miserable conclusion.

William Dove in the death cell.
(York Art Gallery & Museums Trust)

DISCOVERIES

Father Henry Lytherland, 2 August 1538

In a recent booklet, *The Priest Who Defied the King* by M.J. Carty, we have an example of a York story which had been lying in obscure local history for many years, only now brought to general notice as a dramatic tale from the age of Henry VIII.

This is the story of Father Henry Lytherland, a scholarly churchman who studied at Oxford, becoming a Doctor of Canon Law and with this expertise, took the role of adviser on law to Lincoln Cathedral. Lytherland was also connected with Newark and had parishes in North Lincolnshire at Alkborough and at Belton. He was born in 1487 and began his Oxford studies when he was fifteen. He studied for fourteen years at university before entering the world of controversy, fear and rebellion that was Tudor England in the 1530s.

The Pilgrimage of Grace in 1536, and the earlier Lincolnshire Rising, had made it clear to Henry that his destruction of the monasteries and his intolerable taxations and depredations across the land were leading to trouble in the streets and in the villages. Yorkshire and Lincolnshire became a focus for a time, with men like Robert Aske (*see* chapter 2) paying the ultimate penalty for revolt.

We now know that Lytherland spoke openly in church and elsewhere against Henry's repressive regime. Among the oppressive legislation he introduced was the Act of Supremacy of 1534, which made Henry VIII 'the only supreme head on earth of the Church in England' in which he usurped the place of the Pope. Then came the Act of Suppression of 1536, enacted in response to the King's need to destroy the smaller religious houses. This took the draconian measure of grabbing for the Crown all religious houses whose yearly income was more than £200. Lytherland was one of the men who stood firm by Rome and made it clear that he saw the need for strong voices of dissent.

Lytherland's friends, who had expressed similar views of rebellion – Augustine Webster and others – were hounded down and killed. Webster, who had been the prior of a Carthusian House at Belton, near Epworth (later the home of the Wesleys), was arrested and taken to be hanged, drawn and quartered at Tyburn, London. Lytherland's turn came after he had celebrated Mass at St Mary Magdalene's Church at Newark. He was accused of speaking against the King as the new head of the Church of England, and also of participating in the Pilgrimage of Grace.

Henry Lytherland was taken to York, where he was dragged to the scaffold, hanged and then butchered into quarters; his body parts buried in different places. It is one of the most obscure York stories, and is surely one of the most heroic to come from that age of paranoia, when the crime of treason was all too easily committed, sometimes through sheer annoyance and irritation with the tyrannical sovereign, Henry VIII.

A priest being led to execution. (Martyrs to the Catholic Faith, 1878)

APPENDIX

Other hangings at York

Many hangings at York have no records other than a name and an offence. Sometimes there is no clear statement of the offence in question either, merely a forgotten name. This is a list of those not covered in the preceding pages of people executed by hanging at the scaffold. The main sources have been lists done for the Yorkshire Archaeological Society and from the volume by William Knipe, *The Criminal Chronology of York Castle* (1867).

DATE	NAME	CRIMINAL OFFENCE
1379	Edward Hewison	rape
1488	William Babbington John Chambres Thomas Croft Henry Jackson Henry Thompson John Willis	murder
1537	William Wode	heresy
1541	Sir John Nevill & ten retainers	insurrection
1549	Thomas Dale	insurrection
1573	Robert Alcock & ten others	insurrection
1575	Thomas Conrat Fred Gotfried	coining
1577	Henry Mason Robert de Scheveral John de Tradescant	intent to murder
1578	William de Boyle	murder
1579	Hannah Foureroy Charlotte Morrett Charles de Pascal George de Priestley Thomas de Waltire	housebreaking
1581	James Richardson	murder
1582	George Foster	coining
1583	Peter Clark	murder
1583	Rinion Foster	coining
1584	Henry Genremye	robbery
1584	John Jackson	robbery
1585	Thomas de Alasco	coining

1585	George de Kirwan	coining
1586	George de Abbot } William de Abbot	attempted murder
1587	Andrew Turner	coining
1588	Henry Aske	rape
1590	Peter de Ramus	robbery
1590	George Wynch	robbery
1592	Richard Bourboulon } Anthony Hodson Joseph de Hamel	housebreaking
1594	Richard Craw	murder
1595	William de Allestry } Thomas de Allix Robert de Hammond	coining
1596	Henry de Alms	passing bad money
1597	John de Nelme	intent to murder
1598	Thomas de Alting } Robert Swedier	housebreaking
1599	John Taylor	horse-stealing
1599	John Milburn	coining
1602	Charles Beaumond } Thomas Bennington Mary Blakey Emma Brown	coining
1603	William Pennington	murder
1603	Harris Rosenberg	murder
1604	Elizabeth Bradwith } Jane Buckle Hannah Bulmer Richard Cullingworth	coining
1607	Stephen Dobson	murder
1608	Fred Wrightson	murder
1612	Thomas Armstrong } Richard Carson	coining
1613	William Grame	robbery
1613	Thomas Barker } Mark Barnard Philip Darling Rose Dutton Thomas Easingwold Emma Fountain Maria Fowler Mary Robinson	coining
1615	Robert Martinson	robbery
1615	Mark Trumble	robbery
1616	Thomas Pridham	murder
1616	Henry Musgrave } George Ridley	coining

1617	Simon Routledge	horse-stealing
1618	Mark Addison	murder
1620	Robert Hall	coining
1622	George Bell	forging a will
1623	Mark Dunn	murder
1623	Mary Fletcher	murder
1623	Ralph Raynard	murder
1623	Joseph Hetherington	horse-stealing
1624	Richard Bell	coining
1625	Amos Armstrong	horse-stealing
1625	Richard Ridley	horse-stealing
1627	William Cawan	attempted murder
1628	Robert Storey	arson
1630	Charles Rochester George Rocliffe Christopher Singleton Henry Smelt	coining
1634	Thomas Jefferson Charles Hopkinson William Hornby Ben Hornsey Peter Kibblewhite George Kilvington William Kitching Tom Langdale Tom Lazenby Thomas Wardle	rioting
1634	Elizabeth Jackson	poisoning
1634	Owen Thomson	horse-stealing
1638	Henry Aske	intent to murder
1639	Robert Skelton	forgery
1641	John Taylor	arson
1644	John Dove Joseph Dunning Thomas Empson John Robinson Thomas Robinson	robbery
1648	Ebenezer Moore	highway robbery
1649	George & Maria Merrington	murder
1650	George Harrison	uttering bad money
1650	Mary Pope	coining
1650	Richard Thomas	coining
1650	Ann Crowther	poisoning
1652	Elizabeth Anderson Mary Ellison Luke Hinderson George Johnson	robbery

1654	Marmaduke Holmes	stealing fifteen sheep
1656	Jonathan Bramall	uttering coin
1659	Charles Spooner	murder
1660	Michael Reynard Thomas Reynolds Richard Sinop Oliver Williams Henry Hutchinson Francis Mitchell Robert Noke James Norrison Richard Thomas Thomas Wilson George Wolstenhulme	smuggling/murder
1661	Richard Gardener	coining
1661	Jerry Balderson Richard Souly	robbery/cutting off nose of victim
1661	Anthony Beedam	murder of wife
1664	Reuben Beverage	robbery
1665	George Dagnall Robert Snowden	horse-stealing
1668	Ben Ambrose	murder
1668	George Habbishaw	murder
1670	William Vasey	murder
1672	Robert Duffield	arson
1672	Mark Edmund	arson
1673	Miles Beckett	coining
1673	Jane Thompson	coining
1674	Amos Cropper	murder
1678	Mark Dovenor	arson
1680	Andrew Tucker	highway robbery, robbed the mail
1682	Eli Hodges	rape
1684	Nat Pickett	scuttling a brig
1685	John Mortimer	burglary
1686	Mary Cotnam	murdering her daughter
1688	Quinton Hurworth Robert Myers Will Pashley	murder
1690	Henry Kilvington	robbery
1690	William Borwick	murder
1691	Thomas Darnborough	attempted murder
1691	Mark Grayston	robbery
1692	Charles Dimmey	forgery of a will
1692	Hannah Wilkinson	murdering her child
1694	John Collens	sacrilege
1695	Nelson Campion	robbery
1697	Martin Burrell	horse-stealing

1698	John Blackburn	coining
1699	Peter Arundel	maiming
1729	William Bryant Robert Wheat }	horse-stealing
1729	William Parkinson	'murdering a Scotchman'
1730	John Chapello	horse-stealing
1730	Abraham Powell	cutting cloth off tenters
1730	Joseph Askwith John Freeman Richard Freeman }	robbery
1739	John Stead	horse-stealing
1740	William Spink	horse-stealing
1741	George Bainton	forging a will
1741	John Barker	burglary
1741	Joseph Tyson	burglary
1741	John Wright	murder
1749	Thomas Brown	stealing a mare
1749	Robert Fawthorpe	murder
1749	Josiah Fearn	murder
1750	Joseph Garbutt Abraham Scott John Tiplady }	horse-stealing
1752	Ben Farmery	housebreaking
1752	Robert Loveday	housebreaking
1753	David Harkness	horse-stealing
1753	Bezaliel Knowles	murder (only 17 years old)
1753	Edward Wells	forgery
1753	Thomas Downing	sheep stealing
1753	John Wentworth	theft
1753	William Smith	murder (of six relatives)
1754	Francis Jefferson	housebreaking
1754	Joseph Riddell	murder
1756	David Evans John Holdsworth Elijah Oaks Richard Varley }	burglary
1757	George Trotter	murder
1757	Thomas Cooper	horse-stealing
1758	George Berry Matthew Bilton Robert Cole Richard Ford Will Watson }	Riot. 'The Wensleydale rioters'
1759	Henry Nelson	Perjury and forgery
1759	Ben Windle	housebreaking
1759	Ben Hoult	horse-stealing

1759	John Cockburn William Cockburn }	burglary
1761	Ann Richmond	arson
1767	Richard Clark Matthew Young }	robbery
1767	Richard Boys Thomas Boys }	robbery
1768	Leonard Howson	stealing letters from Doncaster post office
1768	Joseph Hall	coining
1768	Joseph Still	coining
1769	Valentine Bailey	murder of an exciseman
1770	David Hartley James Oldfield }	coining
1770	Michael Naylor	murder
1771	Luke Atkinson	murder
1771	John Wright	robbery
1772	Thomas Lawrence	stealing and deserting
1772	John Lazenby	murder
1773	William Fisher	housebreaking
1774	George Belt	housebreaking
1775	William Bean	robbery
1775	Capt. John Bolton	murder (said to have strangled a servant with a fife. Hanged himself in York Castle)
1775	George Bulmer	wife-murder
1775	Francis Jefferson	burglary
1777	James Rice	murder
1781	William Mayers	murder of a bailiff
1781	Joseph Linwood	theft
1782	John Cockcroft	coining (only a shilling)
1783	John Riley	robbery
1784	Lydia Dickensen	child murder
1784	Benjamin Wood	horse-stealing
1784	William Asquith	sheep-stealing
1784	Thomas Knapton	sheep-stealing
1785	Joseph Clough	stealing
1785	William Riley	robbery from the person
1785	John Beck	arson
1785	Matthew Mason	breaking into a church
1785	Robert Smithson	sheep-stealing
1785	Charles Spencer	horse-stealing
1786	Joseph Hartley Robert Watson }	highway robbery
1786	James Proctor	uttering

1787	William Bryan	stealing money and clothes
1787	Daniel Goldthorpe	stealing cloth
1787	John Moretti	murder
1787	Timothy O'Brien	horse-stealing
1787	John Thompson	cattle-stealing
1787	Thomas West	horse-stealing
1788	James Ashforth	sheep-stealing
1788	John Easlewood	sheep-stealing
1788	Thomas Greenwood	housebreaking
1788	Joseph King	uttering
1788	David Lord	housebreaking
1788	Elijah & Joseph Pulleyn }	robbery with violence
1788	Catherine Savage	stealing clothes (husband transported for life)
1789	George Lockley	murder
1789	Robert Wilkinson	robbery with violence
1789	John Barker	housebreaking
1789	Hannah Whiteley	poisoning a child
1790	Henry Bell James Ferguson William Howson }	sheep-stealing
1790	Robert Cramman	horse-stealing
1794	William Waddington	counterfeiting
1794	Thomas Kirk	rape
1795	Charles Elliott	murder
1795	William Brammam William Brittain William Jackson Thomas Mann }	burglary
1795	George Fawcett	sheep-stealing
1797	Robert Dyson	stealing letters
1798	Peter Buck Robert Hollingworth George Ledger }	highway robbery
1798	William Larkin	forgery
1799	Richard Clegg	murder
1800	Elizabeth Johnson	uttering a forged note
1801	Sam Lundy	stealing a cow
1801	James Doughty Richard Holliday }	sheep-stealing
1801	Thomas Hodgson	uttering a forged note
1801	George Sedgewick	uttering a forged note
1801	Edward Tattersall	uttering a forged note
1803	John Mansfield	attempted rape and robbery
1808	Thomas Allington	robbery

1812	William Chester	housebreaking
1813	John James	stabbing a bailiff
1814	Henry Sutcliffe	forgery
1816	James Ord	cutting and maiming
1817	Michael Pickles	murder
1817	James Dearing	rape
1817	Isaac Bradshaw	rape
1817	Ben Gartside	burglary
1817	Ben Micklewaite	burglary
1818	Sam Leatherhead	uttering bad notes
1820	William Kettlewell Charles Puncheon }	housebreaking
1821	Will Thompson	wife-murder
1821	Will Brown	murder
1821	James Bennett	highway robbery
1821	Will Buck	highway robbery
1821	James Butterworth	burglary
1821	James Law	burglary
1821	George Smith	rape
1823	Will Johnson	murder
1823	Robert Gill	stealing from a shop
1823	James Ramsden	stealing
1824	Moresire Camfield	burglary
1824	Michael White	burglary
1825	Richard Holderness	intent to murder
1826	Leonard Wilkinson	murder
1828	John Coates Matthew Harrison John Morrot }	horse-stealing
1830	Joseph Slater	child murder
1832	William Hodkin	rape
1839	Thomas Musgrave	rape
1840	James Bradley	patricide
1841	John Burlinson Charles Gill Henry Nuttall }	murder
1844	Joseph Dobson	patricide
1844	William Hendrew	murder
1848	Patrick Reid	murder
1848	Michael Stokes	murder
1849	George Hone	murder (of his daughter)

BIBLIOGRAPHY

BOOKS

Bland, James, *The Common Hangman*, Zeon Books, 2001
Carty, M.J., *The Priest Who Defied the King*, self-published, 2007
Cyriax, Oliver, *The Penguin Encyclopaedia of Crime*, Penguin, 1993
Davies, Owen, *Murder, Magic, Madness*, Pearson Longman, 2005
Duff, Charles, *A Handbook on Hanging*, Nonsuch, 2006
Evans, Stewart P., *Executioner: The Chronicles of James Berry*, Sutton 2004
Fielding, Steve, *The Hangman's Record: Volume One 1868-1899*, Chancery House, 1999
Henson, Keith, *Foul Deeds and Suspicious Deaths in York*, Wharncliffe, 2003
Knipe, William, *A Criminal Chronology of York Castle*, Burdekin, 1889
Malcom, I., *The Luddites*, Archon, 1970
Newman, P.R., *The Royal Castle of York*, York Museums, 2005
Peacock, A.J., ed., *Essays in York History*, York Education Settlement, 2003
Rede, Thomas Leman, *York Castle*, J. Saunder, 1829
Taylor, R.V., *Yorkshire Anecdotes*, Whittaker, 1889

NEWSPAPERS

The *Hull Packet*
The *Times*

Other titles published by The History Press

Hanged at Durham
STEVE FIELDING

Until hanging was abolished in the 1960s, Durham Gaol was the main centre of execution for convicted killers from all over the north east. It's history began with the hanging of two labourers in 1869, by the notorious hangman William Calcraft. Over the next ninety years a total of seventy-seven people took the short walk to the gallows – including poisoner Mary Cotton, army deserter Brian Chandler, and Carlisle murderer John Vickers.

978 07509 4750 3

Hanged at Pentonville
STEVE FIELDING

The history of execution at Pentonville began with the hanging of a Scottish hawker in 1902. Over the next sixty years the names of those who made the short walk to the gallows reads like a who's who of twentieth-century murder. They include the notorious Dr Crippen, Neville Heath, and mass murderer John Christie of Rillington Place. Steve Fielding has fully researched all these cases and they are collected together here in one volume for the first time.

978 07509 4950 7

Hanged at Liverpool
STEVE FIELDING

Taking over from Kirkdale House of Correction as the main centre of execution for Liverpool, a total of sixty-two murderers paid the ultimate penalty at Walton Gaol. They include Blackburn child-killer Peter Griffiths, whose guilt was secured following a massive fingerprint operation, and Liverpool's Sack Murderer George Ball; as well as scores of forgotten criminals: soldiers, gangsters, teenage tearaways, cut-throat killers and many more.

978 07509 4751 0

Square Mile Bobbies: The City of London Police 1839–1949
STEPHEN WADE

Between 1839 and 1949 the City of London Police were involved in a succession of major cases, from the attempted assassination of the Rothschilds in 1862, to Jack the Ripper's brutal killing of Catherine Eddowes in 1888 and the notorious Siege of Sidney Street in 1911. This chronicle of violent deaths, robberies, forgeries and fraudsters in Britain's capital is a fascinating look at the social history of the City Police in the chronicles of crime.

978 07509 4952 1

If you are interested in purchasing other books published by The History Press, or in case you have difficulty finding any History Press books in your local bookshop, you can also place orders directly through our website:

www.thehistorypress.co.uk